The Willing Observer

K L WICKS

© MKW Publishing

2015

3rd EDITION

Copyright © K L Wicks 2015

The right of K L Wicks to be identified as the author of this work has been asserted in accordance with sections 77 and 78 of the Copyright Designs and Patents Act 1988.

All rights reserved. No part of this publication may be reproduced, stored in a retrieval system, or transmitted, in any form or by any means without the written permission of the publisher, nor be otherwise circulated in any form of binding or cover other than that in which it is published and without a similar condition being imposed on the subsequent purchaser.

In the finest of moments
We can find ourselves
In the darkest of moments
We can know ourselves
Truly.

KNOWLEDGE, MOTIVE & INTENTION

I had to work out some very basic things about myself before I knew I could find happiness. It meant looking at what I was, what made me tick and what I wanted out of life and naturally this led me to some key objectives. In your pursuit for knowledge about yourself or the world around you, don't miss the obvious. Stop to look around once in a while and learn to actually appreciate the ignorance that surrounds you in daily life. Otherwise you cannot possibly hope to learn anything.

Don't look down on ignorance or pretend it doesn't exist; we all suffer from it and are all prone to it, we all start our lives with it and are taught to dispel it as we learn, grow and allegedly mature. But with knowledge and ignorance one cannot exist without the other, information is constantly available, it finds you and feeds you but are you still sleeping? I was. Have you woken up and opened your eyes to the world around you? It was a real shock to me when I did. No-one else can make you learn or understand really what drives you. No one can take control of your life for you, although some will try and rely on others for this or expect it from them. They can merely give you the tools and materials

to try and work it out, hoping you survive and maybe find happiness along the way.
The very first thing I needed to decipher in my unquiet mind to find happiness was what my motive was. I realised it was where everything started. What were my intentions and requirements for fulfilment and satisfaction? I am driven to dream of the darker side of society that we are not allowed to talk about, and had felt like I couldn't indulge these wants or talk about them for what seemed like an age. Well, by understanding what created them is what led me to resolve the conflict they caused within me, to have my cake and eat it if you will. There has to be something to learn in the pursuit of anything, it is a waste of intelligence to not experience the wonderment of knowledge.

Knowledge can be useless though unless it is appreciated and used for experience, which in itself creates more learning. A demanding yet rewarding effort for the person who puts in the time, but it really had come down to a starting point question for me. What do I want? It sounds very selfish when put so plainly but it actually is the height of selfishness. And you must ask yourself this, just as I did.

It may seem to us that there are no new ideas left, that there is no room to be a revolutionary anymore so you must be content with the system of control and the ideology of freedom as it is or as you have come to see it. I dismiss this as stagnant unprogressive thinking that must not be believed. Ideas and thoughts are what make us, define us, change is what evolves us and brings us into new eras of discovery. There is a new free thinking consciousness evolving and secretly marching, of new ideas and beliefs covering the globe but revolution has always found resistance. It will encounter ambush and treachery at every turn, sometimes from your own sensibility, but we must persist in our ideas to show force of mind and conviction in our beliefs.

I find judgement and self-deprecation can be an ugly combination, acknowledging what your weakness is does not mean it has to de-motivate you. Stay true to yourself. By allowing someone else to tell you how to live your life when you know instinctually they are wrong, will lead to living the lie that consumes you in the dark. You must judge yourself and yourself alone, once you believe in yourself you can help others. Although it may start alone, you need others to help finish it.

THE BEGINNING OF ME

To find myself in what one could only describe as a self-constructed drama bordering on crisis was a most peculiar feeling and one I had never actually experienced before or thought I would ever end up in. Although upon reflection I should have seen it coming, recognised what I was doing and had done to get there. It had been hiding in the background of my life for quite some time, gnawing away at my sense of self every day, gradually taking away my soul and what I essentially was. Married life had worn me down and made me forget what my purpose was and what made me happy, although possibly I had never really known and had distracted myself with what society dictated so I could fit in and sleep my way through life.

But that moment of realisation, when the fog lifted and I could see my life clearly, was an earth shattering feeling for me. To finally wake from the half slumber of semi-conscious self-denial felt almost unreal, as if I couldn't possibly be in the waking world and must still be very much dreaming. I felt an awakening so clear it changed everything I had ever known or ever thought about myself and life, the game had changed and I knew there was no going back. It was like a lifetime plan had come together without me knowing it was

coming, and was running itself through to that point of no return and taking me with it.
Because if I had realised, if I had accepted what I needed to do before I was ready, then maybe I wouldn't have played my part as I should. My self-preservation instinct had taken over and steered me down the path I needed to go. Seeking to bring together the creative and the logic which had been at warring conflict within my mind for so long, to make them unite and work together without it being my choice anymore. For the new chapter to begin in my life, the study, science, emotion and empiricism would now influence me and give me what I sought; it just didn't leave room for anyone else at that time.

Breaking this realisation to my spouse however, was an entirely different matter. I had lived the lie I thought I never would, staying in a dead marriage and continuing the charade on auto pilot, not feeling what I should, not saying what I should and not getting what I wanted. I thought I could live with my decision, my mistake, and did for a time but once the blinkers were off I had to accept and do what I knew was right for me and by default, her too. I had carried along an almost innocent bystander who was now caught in the wake of my breakthrough of self. An unfortunate product of a mis-guided soul, I wouldn't say blameless though, it takes two to complete the lie usually but unfortunate none the less. I had never intended to hurt her unnecessarily but can see now that she perpetuated our unhappy marriage as did I for ease of comfort and familiarity. And although she was not ready for the self-denial to be lifted, it had to happen for both our sakes and futures.

Our general lack of communication had led to distance and separation long before either of us admitted to it. I could tell on reflection we had both avoided the conversation for an age, no one wants to be the one to call it for what it was. Just two lonely people sharing the same space, who were still vaguely friends but drifting further apart the longer it continued. Both our lives on different paths but meeting every now and again to let us carry on believing we were happy enough to get by. Ending the relationship that I had been in for a substantial part of my life was hard, I knew we didn't love each other, but weirdly enough I thought she would admit it and knew it too. She apparently didn't. I hadn't quite comprehended I would have to fight for my freedom, not physically but my god she made me fight mentally.

In her profession she made good enough money to survive but had her own issues of abandonment and a fear of being alone which had made me stay for so much longer than I should have. It was what had stopped me leaving previously when we had once discussed the distance and lack of attention she showed me, she said then that she would stop being so insular and depressed but nothing changed within our relationship, so eventually I changed.

I did almost give in a couple of times when she pulled the emotional blackmail routine of how she would change and we could be so happy together if I would only give it another chance. I had been there before and knew she was clutching at straws and that I had to hold fast to my new way of thinking when faced with the actual pain it was causing. It was so hard to see someone you once loved so completely crushed and scared but I had waited a long time for this to be real and wouldn't let it go without the necessary fight. I felt excitement and pending freedom with my decision and I naively wanted her to feel the same. With clarity of mind came clarity of explanation as well. I was able to counsel her in the adjustment of it all, to help her reconcile herself with the loss and subsequent grieving period that followed.

I put my own new found feelings and want for living on hold for a short while longer to absolve myself from this pain she was trying to inflict upon me. I felt it was my duty, to leave as little mess behind as I could. I was not intending to take anything but positivity from this experience and wanted the same for my soon to be ex-wife although I wasn't under any delusions, I knew it wasn't that easy for her despite my efforts. After a month I had to back off, I realised she was becoming dependent on my attention where she never actually had been throughout our marriage, creating a new strange bond of friendship and support that was for her benefit and not mine, defeating the object of the exercise in my view.

I was just not prepared to compromise after so long hidden in the shadows, which left me with no choice other than to walk away. We didn't have any children together, I owned the house and had my own practice so didn't really have to change much on the face of it and she had to move out and start again. She was facing rejection, fear of the unknown and standing on her own two feet. Upheaval and change are difficult for anyone and I had had more time to get used to this idea, even if it was only a few days or weeks longer, it still appeared easier for me to adjust to the new thinking and freedom I had. I was just not willing to conform anymore, especially just for the sake of my marriage.

Conforming for society's sake had driven me to the brink of sanity I thought, but as the shroud was lifted, I saw the truth. Everyone was conforming, hiding, running from a fear in their minds, different torments, different secrets and different fears. It was astounding to see, to suddenly understand we are all hiding because everyone is hiding. It seemed so simple and ridiculous at the same time I laughed out loud. I knew I must break the mould and take the leap of faith to believe that there is another life for me, a better life for what I want. And it doesn't need to hurt anyone, by my standards, and that is what counted now, my standards. After all, it was my life and I could make myself happy. I mean, that's what it's all about isn't it? To be happy?

To realise your true potential can take an awfully long time if you didn't know you were looking for it and just as long even for someone who thought they knew they were. I should imagine there are those among us who are blessed enough to know already, but as a general rule, most do not, have not or cannot. Due to self, outside influence or continuous distractions, many do not even seek it; instead electing to subconsciously fear it. And rightly so, it can be a frightening thing to imagine living a life as you. Being who you truly wanted and wanting what you truly can have feels unbelievably selfish and fantastic all at the same time. I know now I afforded too much stigma to the word 'selfish' previously, but it actually is the basis for happiness in my world now and is a two way street if you are in a relationship.

I know the difference between right and wrong, I chose my side and now I just had to live it. Society was not imposing anything on me, merely providing the construct for the delusion to continue if I so wished; I had done this to myself and accepting this knowledge is what changed everything. Taking the blame and recourse for my own existence and mistakes, accepting I was my own person and only I made my ultimate decisions was essential. The basic fear and anxiety I had felt towards life changed then, to excitement with a hint of what I might call happiness in the near future and it was just too tempting to turn away from. I was willing to take on a life of potential loneliness and misery in place of my stable, comfortable current situation. It seemed like madness to everyone else, especially my wife, I knew it did, but the feeling and temptation was strong and unyielding. I knew what had to be done and did it, it started with a feeling but logic and reason were now driving me forwards in my pursuit of a strangely long lost dream that had always been there in the depths of my mind.

I obviously didn't explain all of my motives and intentions to my wife though; it began to open a can of worms and led to a deviation from the point. Which was future happiness being possible for me and not dwelling on past un-fulfilment. This was a bitter pill to swallow for the other party I found; it's hard to not insult someone when you are telling them they can't make you happy and had their chance. And then reasoning it with because they just aren't what you want anymore. It sounds extremely valid in your own mind but when the words are released there must be more to follow to back up your reasoning. I didn't have all the answers at that point. I was just going on a feeling, which was most unlike me. I was being ruled by my heart and not my head for a change, it felt refreshing and incredibly frightening all at once. It was hard and I was pushed almost to breaking point during those sessions of intense discussion but retained my focus and beliefs of myself. I had to. It took time and patience but I got my freedom and could finally begin the new life I had only had a taster of previously and spent years imagining until now.

I had no idea what I would be unleashing or stepping into when I discovered myself. I felt like a small child in a sweet shop with unlimited funds, I didn't know where to start or what to indulge in first without having that instinctual awful feeling of what if someone finds out. I was still shedding the societal teachings of what is apparently acceptable and what one should and shouldn't do. That was gradually fading away, it didn't matter what anyone else thought anymore. It was about being honest with my own self first and foremost, if I wasn't even doing that then I had no chance at happiness now or ever.

The only way I could really understand myself or what could be achieved from my deepest darkest desires and experiences so far meant going back. Working my way back through what lay at the foundations of the man I am today. Through all the pivotal moments, the choices and the wonderings to see where it would all lead me in the end. Although I had had my own awakening, I realised and knew it still wasn't the type of subject one could discuss in an open situation or forum unless you find similar minded people. I believe you are either invited to 'special parties' or may be referred to a special therapist when openly discussing sexual desires, deviances or torments in today's society. Although those therapists are some of the most repressed and most deviant people I have ever met and really don't inspire one to talk openly about sexual interest of any nature.

This type of journey is a very personal one to each who undertakes it, I did not have the need to discuss my life or goals with a professional stranger, it would take them too long to understand where I was now, I didn't have that time. I needed to get started right away on working it all out, I had my suspicions of course and I did not walk into this task blindly, but it can take a lifetime to know yourself and still one can miss it. I knew there was much work that needed to be done.

I realised that wants and desires may have been driving this train, but it was created over many years, from many assumptions and much input about life, dreams, hopes and fears. Mine and other peoples. Perspectives can and had changed, on both sides, so I tried not to get disillusioned along the way about what I was really doing, instead seeing the journey for what it was. Feeling it for what it is. A life experience. I wondered if I could make the adjustments, make the changes that may compromise my own ideals and morals and that may raise questions of my own beliefs and standards and expectation of myself and life. I felt I had to. I couldn't stop this juggernaught now I had set it in motion, but knew I could either get on for the ride and see where it took me, or crash and burn and go back to a life of borderline misery hidden in complacency.

I knew then that reality would be what I made it, not what people were expecting from me or for me. If it feels wrong, change or fix it, only I knew. And that instinctual feeling continued to drive me. It's just not always that easy to explain to someone else who may feel very differently to you or not comprehend where you are in your life and how you got there. And how did I get here? I had to ask myself this very question. So I went back, worked my way through from the early beginning to find the markers and the moments that defined my thoughts and wants. It was a revelation to my mind to clearly analyse what had previously gone overlooked but was so obviously important to my way of being.

CHILDHOOD PLAYGROUND

I think I first realised that I liked watching when I was about eight years old. It was in the playground; well from the detention room actually I could see the playground. I had not had detention before and was extremely miffed at missing the outside time I loved so much after being stuck inside for hours trying to concentrate on a boring presentation of facts from my teacher. But, rather than being given lines as punishment on these detentions we were made to just sit and watch the other children having fun hoping to serve as a learning experience of behaving and our first real lesson in conforming by means of segregation. To instil the ability to do as we were told or miss out. It was a very simple yet effective methodology to follow and yielded instant results from most students who didn't find themselves in detention very often. Yet there would always be the impulsive few who lacked the self control or conformist gene if there is such a thing, and would find a regular spot reserved even though the process had obviously failed for their type of mindset.

To concentrate on writing lines at this young age didn't seem to have the desired effect the establishment were looking for, which is why they found a different approach. But I did not suffer from the feeling of exclusion they were trying to make me feel. For me it gave me the valuable time

I needed and didn't rightly find as a child to actually just watch. I was constantly running, moving and thinking which made it difficult to stop and just take in the world. Funny really when I always thought it should be the time you are watching and learning the most, but miss so much. Without the experience to know what to look for or it passes us by to be thought about a long time later if remembered at all.

But this day was different, I had all the time in the world to just sit and stare. Had been given a window into my own childhood for a moment, got to watch the unfolding break time and all the players, each group doing their own thing. A few boys kicking a football, girls with skipping ropes and jumping on one leg in that weird mystical game called hopscotch that all girls and only girls know. But everyone found a role in these crucial breaks to the monotony of the school day.

But my experience of detention was quite different. I watched, just staring and allowing my mind to go where it wanted to. Before long the staring turned to wondering and my brain came alive with many imaginings. This gave me a curious feeling, one of immense power because they didn't know I was watching them, the girls didn't know I had caught a glimpse of knickers as the wind had blown and caught someone off guard for a second. Didn't know I was imagining chasing one of them so I could grab a kiss. The imaginings and thoughts this triggered stayed with me forever, my very first awakening and awareness of my place in this world starting to form.

I felt I had found two things simultaneously, a love of study and my chosen subject matter, even from a young age this gave me a sense of purpose.
The next four or five formative years produced many encounters and games both on playground and estate that only served to fuel my interest in viewing the opposite sex and my yearning to control them sexually. Games like kiss chase, hide and seek and doctor and patient (I found doctors and nurses too equal!), definitely fuelled my interest and gave adequate opportunities for one on one contact. Many times resulting in the pinning down of girls who would appear to, for all manner and purposes actually enjoy it and be getting a thrill at being dominated just as I was at being the dominator. I did not miss this insight at the time, but only with a childish comprehension did I take it on board. I analysed it as best I could and noted everything in my mind, often replaying those moments and wondering what could have transpired had I been more astute.

Of all the games that children play, Hide and Seek was always my favourite if I'm honest, that was a hunt your prey exercise for me, but always inevitably resulted in only a quick snog and a grope in a cupboard if I was lucky. I knew the boundaries, everybody did, we were taught the usual social rules surrounding sex and had to work out the rest for ourselves from each other or by mis-judging a situation and learning the hard way. I always prided myself on being a bit cleverer and more observant than the rest of my peers, this didn't win me any friends but it got me what I wanted, to be left alone to get on with my own agenda. I felt I took the time to watch and listen; I paid attention, to everything around me and reaped the benefits. I was also a keen observer of who was watching me, where people went, what times things happened, regularity of routine and how these things may affect my musings and instinctively knowing they were important. I was not taught to be observant and calculating, it just happened naturally.

I was still quite disillusioned though, I was a child. I understood the playing field as far as my age group and maybe a couple of years above and below me but I had no concept of the 'grown up' world. I believed naively that they had everything planned and knew exactly what was going on and where they were going. This oversight or lack of understanding is only natural for a child or young adult, but when I realised they don't have all the answers, I took it as a massive failure on my part, to not see the whole world as it was and to have allowed myself a false sense of security. It shook my confidence greatly at the time and I then spent years trying to make up for it before I understood that everyone else was making it up as they went along too.

I internally punished myself for being either too involved or too separated, not able to assimilate the emotional and the logical to work together as one. I couldn't quite grasp analysing a situation while going through it, instead electing to be distant and outside what should be a personal experience for the sake of study. I know now that this was due to a combination of me growing up, my thought process beginning to form and of trying to understand myself. It was about the brain developing and learning new experiences, but it felt again like failure at the time when I did not seem to see or feel things as others did. But I did not always take this failure as defeat.

EARLY GAMES

There were a number of games in childhood that developed my interest in stalking and domination. Games where it was easy to the separate girls from each other or to lead them away from prying eyes. Our school grounds made it easy to wander off on break and not be seen, to walk round the back to the dark shaded area with a shy girl in tow becoming vaguely aware of what this was. This was probably the initial onset of the need for a fear response I supposed later, for her hand to try and slightly pull away from mine so she could back away. My grip tightens, she's is staying. I couldn't possibly have understood all the significances of these events at the time but have spent years after re-analysing them to gain the meaning and lessons they represented.

Although she tried to pull away and wasn't entirely compliant in the forced fumble that followed, she didn't really protest and allowed it to runs its course. This was the order of childhood and teenage fumblings I assumed. I was however; completely thrown by the fact she appeared quietly keen to spend the next break following me again and had appeared at my side. Again she made a small attempt to retreat at a certain point, making me slightly excited again and this time I moved my hand to grip her wrist and was a bit more forceful than last time. It worked. It was compliant noncompliance I learned much later when I was able to start categorising behaviours. I had never really thought I would be able to indulge my passions or fantasies without getting into trouble or at least having to discuss it with the other party which made me feel very uncomfortable at the thought when I was younger. We had many a fun break time in the dark of the trees and we never did have a conversation in the end, just one final session where I discovered my boundaries were still limitless, hers were not. Games can be for pure fun or can have an extra motive, for study purposes, it's sometimes OK to mix the two but never to the detriment of the experiment or learning experience.

Some classic favourites have always enchanted and intrigued me, hide and seek as mentioned previously being the first. The whole basis of the game is to run and hide, for an assailant to then essentially hunt you and find you. For what they are to find you for is never spoken of. You are never meant to escape though; hope isn't the aim of this game. Inevitability of capture is, and that's the thrill. It really is just a game to separate the girls from each other and to give the boys a chance to have a go I always thought.

Murder in the dark must have also been thought of with this in mind as it is perfectly designed for blatant groping, a certain skill that is further developed later in life by over keen bosses and middle aged drunken men at Christmas parties.

Kiss Chase really does not need an explanation other than both parties are well aware of the games intention. This was only really up until the age of 12 or 13 though, after that a different set of rules suddenly applied and serious hormones changed the goalposts completely. Making the whole thing slightly more serious, confused, intense and dangerous. Generally the order of any teenage life, sexual or not.

All these games gave me so much opportunity to indulge in my budding interests; gave me so much information about the people playing them as well as the people who didn't. One who didn't take part in particular sticks in my mind to this day. Another boy, who I assumed had a demon following him too but possibly a tad darker than mine, would watch but more intently than I did without the ability or want to join in. He noticed me too, but there was an unspoken telepathy thing going on here of malicious intent that made me keep a good distance from him. He was unsettling shall we say, even to me. His appetites lay in a much darker box than mine I soon found out but wished that I hadn't.

Although I stayed out of his way generally, there was an occasion when our paths did cross. One of the rare times I went against my better judgement and instinct out of pure curiosity, and proved why it is a bad idea to do so. A normal summer afternoon on the estate and the usual rapscallion kids causing trouble, worthy distractions for us more devious ones to be getting along with our work. I had been monitoring a subject for a few days when in my still hidden position I noticed my demonised counterpart following a girl a few years younger than us but without being in view of anyone else. I noticed his behaviour change subtly once at a safe distance and I recognised the chase and knew a catch was on.

I felt compelled to follow him, and had to override my gut feeling to move away, to not look back and keep walking now I was on my feet. But I did turn back, I wanted to know. I followed at a discreet distance and watched what his intention really was, wondering if my assessment had been correct or if he really was like me. I had to know I thought. My stance as mere observer rendered me powerless in this operation, I detached myself from being involved by convincing myself I was just a bystander to life and didn't have control over that level of mastery to dictate the future outcome of something so sinister. It was soon clear he was leading her to an old stone bunker on the edge of military property near to our estate. I stayed back enough to be hidden in the surrounding bushes, to see them both disappear into the stone darkness.

I suddenly didn't want to be here, wished I had listened to my feelings and stayed in the safety of my stalking position where I was in control. I decided what happened and what I saw, what I did and how it would play out. Here I was not in control. But I couldn't do anything, my inability to mix logic and emotion was in full swing and I was logically trying to work out what I should do, unable to allow my emotional response centre to take over and guide me. I was actually scared. Quite the new feeling for me, I always went with my instinct and believed in it unquestionably, so the feeling of anxiety that was created by going against it was awful. Once realised I couldn't move and held my position in the bushes unsure of what to do next.

It wasn't long before I heard the girl crying followed by muffled screams and scraping noises. My adrenaline rose instantly but to an alarming level, I thought my heart was pounding so loudly it would give away that I was there and I would have to run. My legs weren't going anywhere though; I was fixated in horror to hear what I could only imagine was happening but wished I couldn't. Struggling with the complexity of my emotions and trying to deal with actual devilry at work was almost too much. I hadn't known how terrible it would be to hear the begging and torture, to hear someone pleading for their life for real. I wanted someone else to come and stop this awfulness, I wished I could have shown some bravery and stepped up as I was there. But no one else was going to come and fear had paralysed me, actual fear for myself too. It sounds so stupid and unsympathetic but it was the first time I had felt empathy and fear and it rendered me useless.

I also suddenly comprehended that this wasn't from the want for control I had. This was something entirely different and I didn't like it, that darker box he lived in was more sinister than I had thought or given credit to. It must have been two hours before he emerged from the bunker, alone. A quick glance left and right and he started away but not the way he had come, actually heading in my direction instead to make it a full circuit and not look like he was heading back from the bunker. I was so low already I didn't think I could hide any better so held my breath instead, hoping it would be enough to make me part of the undergrowth . He wasn't stopping though, with a scarily calm look and confident stride, he left. And I was left alone, aware that I was probably now the only living person remaining at this site.

I knew I needed to check though; I couldn't just walk away, now my instinct had returned I never wanted to go against it ever again and it was telling me I needed to know. There was such a strange feeling as I got close to the bunker, I felt guilt even though I hadn't committed this horror, I hadn't stopped it. I glanced into the doorway and that was enough to get the full picture of what he had done. It was an atrocity, a devastating end for her, raped and tortured to death and then some dismemberment of the body. He was trying to perfect a technique I thought and knew that he would do this again if given the chance. I really didn't want to understand this situation in any capacity but I did. I knew I was a witness but felt more like an accomplice because I didn't do anything to stop it and it would haunt me forever.

My self-preservation mechanism took over at this point and made myself get up and get away, quickly, quietly and not leaving anything behind that might show I was here. I was slightly different after that, it changed and shaped my view on life, control, desire, regret, guilt and empathy in one awful moment. It then took me years to work through all those emotions, to understand that event and all the significances of it, obvious or not.

I stayed out of his way even more after that but luckily he disappeared from school very shortly after the young girl's mutilated body was discovered and he found his way into custody. It was all over the local news and the town had talked about it for months after about if anything could have been done. I quietly carried around my guilt and regret and spoke to no one about what I had seen, I knew better than that. I was glad he got caught though; I could tell he was the obsessed evil type and there was no place in society for that kind of darkness. Possibly not even sexually motivated, but more about the kill and the suffering, they are the ones to watch out for. It may sound weird but I believe a stalker should be sexually motivated by a love of women, otherwise bad things can and do happen.

All of this paved the way for my adult personality to form and develop into the well rounded individual I am today; I just have some kinky and deviant obsessions that developed along the way as well alongside it.

ADOLESCENT PLAYGROUND

As I got older and into adolescence, it was becoming clear to me that I may be in a minority when it came to my sexual interests. I didn't really seem to have many close friends, probably because I preferred watching people rather than talking to them, but had read enough to know that what I envisioned wasn't the norm. The few 'experiences' I had were what I consider now to be extremely lucky escapes and could have really damaged my future just by my lack of understanding of what I had discovered about myself and by not learning enough about other people yet.

I wasn't bad looking and despite not talking much, I did get invited to a few parties here and there. Only when I finally accepted one of these invitations did it become extremely obvious to me just how much watching you can do at them! Well, not just watching. I will explain how the process went and I'm sure still does. The beginning of the evening is a bit tame, a few drinking games, some dancing and laughter as light-hearted banter takes place. As the night progresses and alcohol and other substances are consumed, some of the girls begin to not entirely know where they are or quite remember who they are with. It seems unsporting I know, but as a young man I felt this was just too easy. On a plate one might say. Not quite content with a drunken hussy draped over me making it clear what she was after, I instead went for a wander round the house to see what I could find.

What I did find was a girl, almost passed out on a bed from too much to drink, in the room alone. I can't even describe the feeling I had. Quickly locking the door behind me and leaving the light off, I made my way over to the bed and sat next to her. I wanted her to know I was there, to know she was trapped and that I was in control. There is a moment, the calm before the storm that is when the silent concerto is at its loudest in my mind.

I decided my Direct Approach would probably be prudent, grab of the wrists, straddling the body and kiss, forcefully. It evolved from here but the Direct Approach has been extremely effective over the years and it is easily adaptable to modification depending on reaction (makes a difference if they know you're going to do it!). My first aim was achieved and being in position felt so good, feeling my weight over her and knowing I was in charge. I savoured that split second that seemed to go on forever of just before she reacts. Then a new feeling, adrenaline starts increasing as my muscles tense in natural response to hers trying to push me away and it feels just like I expected it too. Amazing. I lean down and kiss her while the reaction is still forming, wanting to release a hand or try and hold both of hers with one of mine so with a hand free it could go roaming.

There is no fear in my mind, only control. I kissed her again and this is usually the point where you can assume how the rest is going to go. She will either fight and it will be a struggle, or will quietly comply as she knows there is no choice but will still show some resistance if she knows how to play the game right. Fairly easy as the alcohol had rendered her unable to be a fighter on this occasion, but a knock at the door interrupted my ultimate goal. Her friends saying they were leaving, they tried the door and told her she had five minutes to get downstairs. I took this as my call to be going, she wasn't entirely unattended after all and I had had some fun. I was gone and out the back door unseen to go away and mull over my new found confidence and playing field.

It was not the sort of habit I could ever talk about, as I got older still I learnt from society that certain behaviours and interests were inherently wrong, things like stalking, coercion and non-consensual sex. But at least I had a label I could work with, sexual deviant apparently. There were a number of well written psychology journals and studies on the subject which honed my understanding of my 'condition' and gave me the beginnings of working it into my 'normal' life. I had relationships and engaged in regular sexual activities in an attempt to hide what I was or at least pretend I wasn't for appearances. It's really hard living a lie. It consumes you. It made me obsessed with what I wanted and couldn't have and angry that it was society forcing me to tell myself I couldn't have it or live how I wanted. I just decided one day to tell myself I could.

ADULT PLAYGROUND

I made the catastrophic mistake of actually getting married in an attempt to conceal my true nature, to actually deny what I knew I was. Conscious self-denial is a big struggle I can tell you. But once I became free of this self-imposed prison I concentrated on what I wanted, and it was from this time I developed my system of techniques further. I developed the Direct Approach to include handcuffs and introduced some new ones to be tested as the opportunities presented themselves. And they did, that is what I found so startling, that I didn't have to look far for subjects to engage with. There were so many unattended women who seemed to have no regard for their safety or virtue, and men who obviously didn't think like I did or they would also have been watching or aware to guard against me.

One of the tastes that developed with age was allegedly unavailable women, if they were married or in a relationship it really got me. The control was magnified when it was someone else's territory you were invading, a very primal feeling. But they were the ones who instigated it mostly, it's easy to pull married women, to spot the unfulfilled ones as they are always on the lookout and know how to play cloak and dagger. The original sense of the term, I have my own game called cloak and dagger but it is quite different.

They also seem to be looking for a sense of danger, cheating being dangerous enough but if they walk away believing you took liberties with them they are blameless in infidelity (this is termed non-consensual consensual sex and has been used to destroy and save many a marriage in equal measure).

They allowed me to dominate them; they pretended they didn't want it in case ever accused, but really it was all a rouse, so they could get what they wanted. I learnt a great deal about what people really wanted on my travels, how they hide behind the mask of 'reality' to keep the world normal and happy. But no-one actually seemed normal and happy, each person hiding from something and carrying some secret with them. I could see it in all of them.

But it was the weakness in women I chose to prey on. It was their confusion and vulnerability that inspired me and I love them for it. It may seem that I do not respect women, on the contrary, I adore, love and respect women in all their wonder. It may sounds strange to some people but I only prey on women who want to be preyed on. It's an instinctual supply and demand system built up over generations of evolutionary responses and triggers. Extremely human in fact. But most men seem to have forgotten this or have been confused by etiquette and rules, and most women have learnt to repress their true desires. But there are some of us out here indulging these instincts on both sides. During my marriage I had affairs and liaisons with a number of women, who also being trapped in a dead life, gave off a certain look and that was my own personal red flag. If you've seen it you'll know what I am talking about, when they hold your eye for just a second longer than necessary and either blush and or then look directly at their husband to see if they noticed. Usually they do not, that's the point of why they are looking for something else. My wife also seemed oblivious to my wandering eye and mind, stuck in her own constructed play of normality and appearances. I took this as my playing field and gave it my all; playing with someone else's naughty wife definitely had its benefits and rewards.

And this is the playground that still continues in my life today; brining me new pleasures and wants, finding light and dark along the way to enjoy. It just so happens I lean towards the dark more than the light but have learnt so much that it would be a sin in itself to not share it.

THE DISTURBING FACTS AND WOMEN

Aside from the normal picture I have painted so far there is a darker side to my personality and interests that I feel have not been entirely encapsulated yet. It requires a more psychological analysis to give you some of the understanding I have gained about my chosen field of human interactions and carnal pleasures.

For my part, I study women, who they are, how they feel and what they want. During these studies I have obtained much extra knowledge about their general behaviour and mental processes which all help in the ultimate goal of making them mine, but may seem trivial at the time to the ordinary observer. Everything you say and do counts, it all gives away something, and I have just learnt to read between the lines. I am the type of person who likes to have on the ground hands on experience of what I study; to keep my mind occupied as well my sexual appetites. This gives me so much more to work with than what just the exterior provides and can make an experience so much more rewarding. It can also lead to new expectations and understanding of one's own intentions so I always try not to miss the lessons in it for me.

Aside from stalking and my darker obsessions I maintain a healthy stream of one night stands which keeps the flow of information and entertainment steady, occasionally one hour stands but it depends on when the husband or boyfriend is due home, or if out and about. Opportunity can knock in the unlikeliest of places. Hardly any discussion or exchange of words ever takes place with these women; it's done purely on sexual telepathy. I will explain how that occurs more in depth later if you are unfamiliar with the term. There are different types and levels of flirting though, the ones who can't do telepathy for example will, instead elect for verbal instigation. These can be either by direct and blatant chat up lines or by use of hints and suggestions. These days some call them subtle hints, but only because most are too stupid to notice or understand them. To the trained ear though, they are red flags. I'll explain.

Reg Flags – I was amazed how many women discuss their wants and desires in either basic coded fashion or just plain simple English. A bit of eavesdropping or just asking the right questions reveals a lot of information or repression that I could work with. With my motives understood, I knew what I was looking for; it depends on your pleasure though. Also, I have been given information without even having to ask for it on many occasions, it can happen.

It is another language to some, I admit, it's not men's fault they don't know, the goalposts do move now and again. But the basics don't change.

Most women are in need of a good old fashioned 'seeing to', mostly the fault of men, obviously, but there is no reason women can't be equal in every department apart from the bedroom. And most of them know it. They are just as clever, can be as strong, whip the shit out of men when it comes to multi-tasking, running a household and family, work just as hard but, they are not the leader in the bedroom.

I feel lucky I discovered this early on and wasn't left with the questioning so many others have for years, making it difficult to understand being equal and dominated at the same time. Women aren't lesser than me because I can control them behind them closed doors. My power isn't from theirs being diminished, quite the opposite. I get a kick out of knowing someone who may appear to be a control freak and completely in charge was tied up and begging for a pounding not 24 hours ago. That being my previous boss and me being extremely satisfied at such an escapade. I had secret liaisons with many of the female workers in my office, all harbouring slightly different wants and desires but still in denial of their true nature. It was easy to watch them, to get them, once they were on the list, targeted; it was just a matter of time. I found in my main environment there featured three distinct categories of woman.

Mousey Shy Type – Now I determined that these would be the easiest to dominate and have my way with, even possibly help to rid them of what appeared to be obvious repression. I hadn't quite comprehended initially that the repression is not always of a sexual nature and sometimes there are other confidence issues at play or actual mental illness. My quest to cure was soon overtaken by a mission of mercy leading me to the next group.

Flirty Outgoing Type – Surely I would find this group the easiest to gain control with I thought, my ego did occasionally run away with itself, being politely knocked back into shape by reality now and again. These women love the game, the chase, the public flirt and tease, but instantly lose their confidence when cornered. It was almost as if a switch was flicked from bolshie to compliant and they just did as they were told, which was not a problem for me but it did seem to be lacking something.

Driven Confident Types – Now this I knew would be the challenge category and therefore quite an important control group in the overall experiments. Quite aloof, constantly hiding behind ambition and confidence to shield themselves from being a target or falling into a certain industry trap of achieving success. These were the women who required time and effort to break them down, to disassemble them slowly and make them want to submit to my will. Often married in real life but at a minimum to their careers, they were the trophies I sought.

Women as a rule are in denial, mostly. Self denial of some simple truths about what they desire and lust after and what really turns them on. There are plenty of societal influences that affect the denials as well as deep seated issues, resentments and other emotional trauma that seem to follow women around like a shadow.

These are what you must learn to observe, understand and control. How you understand them will not be how they understand themselves, but it's your wants that must be paramount, hers are consequential in the whole affair. If you are happy, then she should be too but it must be earned on both sides. They don't realise that most of the time it has nothing to do with appearances or looks, it's about the energy you are receiving and giving. Women can be distracted by more superficial things than men sometimes; this is where your dominant attitude can set you apart without relying on being traditionally 'good looking', which actually gets you noticed more and can be an occupational hazard for the stalker types.

When we are young, we are at the mercy of nature and ignorance, combined to create a featureless landscape to fill as we learn. We work on instinct as we have no other point of reference for certain things or feelings. We tend to grow out of recognising it as we get older and social impediments take over to skew our instincts and forced boundaries hold us back. This leaves a very confusing playing field for some who are not paying attention.

For the people like me, it gives us so much more to work with. It would be terribly mundane if we all thought alike or could predict everything around us. Women have always been known for their changeability, lack of emotional control, denying primal urges, us and theirs, as well as confusing all concerned with irrational behaviour. All of this is due to self denial, self repression and sometimes just good old fashioned craziness. Workable with apart from the last one. There is a certain type of unhinged that can inspire or provoke something in you that could be uncontrollable; it's a very perilous path to take and once taken you may not make it back from intact.

Working with women can be difficult for me, I could mostly concentrate; efficient working meant more time for watching and the ability to do both was there to a point. But once the imagination really got going though there was no way through it. It would catch me off guard sometimes too, meandering off into some daydream of supply closets and a coerced office girl bent over a copier machine - even the best trained mind can go back to default settings for a minute. So I would quickly turn my attention to my evening plans to refine my musings and to get my brain back to precision and planning. It's much easier to turn back to work mode with that mindset as well, I'm sure many a work hour has been lost through deviant wanderings, real or otherwise.

Inevitably though I would become bored with what was available to me in the workplace and move on to another building, another brand, another broad. A few years of this and I began to feel stagnant, like I had lowered my standards or just wasn't putting in the effort I used to. Maybe I was just lazy. There was so many easy pulls I had forgotten to work for my rewards, I needed a challenge to test my boundaries. I wanted to know how far I would go and knew it was going to be a lone mission from this point on.

MEN

In the study of anything there is usually a bi-product study and mine ended up being men. In watching women, I naturally ended up noticing things about men that contributed to the study, events caused and influenced by them giving me an outsider's view. Having the advantage of being that way minded I found it incredibly easy to ascertain what they were doing and why. This is why I referred to stupidity earlier, not through any disrespect, but through very basic observations proving this to be the case on both sides. I feel it is implied for men to either be disciplinarian in the house and bedroom, or easy going in the house and disciplinarian in the bedroom. But due to not many people actually divulging this information, as it happens behind closed doors, either has to be instinctually recognised or learnt. But as this also doesn't fit in with the women's revolution of equality it has been lost and replaced with more false ideals and taught behaviours.

The relationship between my parents was an interesting one, if not a bit traditional. He worked hard and paid the bills; she ran the house and dreamed of a career but didn't have the education to back it up. I'm sure many people have that same story. But it seemed to create a strange tension in the house I never understood at the time. I had no real concept of broken dreams or unrealised aspirations eating away at you for years so didn't know what it could possibly be from my stance as offspring. Naturally as a child I thought it was me or I had done something wrong so stayed out of the way as much as I could.

Neither were the 'parent' types I realise now, very much going through the society motions of settle, marry, breed, grow old and die. And it doesn't play out for a satisfying life it would appear to me. Yet still I fell into the trap too like so many others, but I had a taster first of what I was leaving behind and I actually think it saved me from that self constructed cage later on. Knowing I could have control over my life and use my skills and intuition for a purpose made it feel worth it. I never questioned my dad on relationships or marriage, even when I got older because I felt it as I was programmed to; I didn't need to ask anyone's approval or whether it was right or wrong, it never occurred to me too. Exactly how it felt later on to have the lies stripped away and know the truth, I felt it and words explained it, I didn't need anyone to confirm it for me.

I didn't spend much social time at school, the few times in the senior years when I had been hanging out reading a few of the lads would stand near me and talk about their frustrating girlfriends or who they apparently had the night before. A few times I nearly felt a pang of guilt (I think it was guilt, not one of the more familiar emotions I must say),

knowing I had cornered one of their girlfriends the previous week and that she had given up more than he was getting.
I knew how to work out girls easily and the senior years were the best of my enforced education days, so much subject matter it was almost overwhelming. For both studies it was a daily barrage of data from all angles and processing it all has taken years really to be honest. But all these conversations and interactions did give me an insight into the insecurities and ignorance of most adolescents. But for men specifically, it was funny how the intelligence levels were not in question, but their ability to understand and communicate with girls and women certainly was.

I understood my abilities to have a standard relationship were impaired by my other tastes and interests by how difficult I found it to talk to anyone about it. This led me to have to make a subconscious decision of sorts to 'put away' certain wants and conform to my understanding of reality at the time. It's strange though that such an important aspect of my life could be apparently discarded so easily and I don't even remember the exact moment I did it; I have a feeling I should have. I suppose if I did then I may have fought harder for it, but that is the subconscious for you, it's sneaky like that, I warn you. But you can't hide who you are forever.

But most men make a mountain out of a molehill when it come to relationships and make what should be the easiest thing in the world a struggle because they listen to what women tell them they should be thinking or feeling. I can only assume incompatibility is an issue in some cases, but for others it's about being not quite sure, and not brave enough to ask or just do.

These days' men are waiting for women to tell them what to do, which completely defeats the object of taking control. Asking a woman when to take control has missed the point entirely, yet this is what they have dictated, and we have let them. To our own detriment I might add. So I refuse to let this be the order for my life and took steps to indulge my instincts and live without repression. Now this is all still behind closed doors you understand, I am a private man and believe that certain lifestyle choices I make should be of no importance to people I know in my daily life.

I find I am aiming to achieve a balance in my life of control and domination against my ordinary conformist compliant self. If my ego gets in the way then I can become too domineering and can find it impedes my ability to see an experience through to a desirable conclusion. It must be for the bigger picture and conceding should not be taken as self defeat. To compromise is to be mature and learned sometimes, be the bigger person.

TYPES OF PREDATOR

Very rarely have I met a predatory male other than myself, but it has happened. I have found there are different levels of predator with many motives behind their mask but I can generally spot the signs. In the darkest case of my adult career I still have a feeling that I saved someone from certain death by intercepting a stalk and kill, and turning it into a stalk and rape. She lived and I felt like I had done my good deed for the day. I know when it's written in black and white like that it sounds so clinical and cold but instincts sometimes can be. Most people should know what category they fall into if they too have interests like mine and indulge in this type of endeavour. But do not confuse this with being a normal opportunistic man; I have seen many a tangled web unfold from not knowing who you really are and what you want. The following are the types of stalker as I personally see them:-

Opportunistic Stalker – I consider these the low grade stalker, green level if you will. It will usually be quick, to the point and generally lack any finesse. They rarely give thought to any real planning and precision, preferring more to work in the moment and not take the valuable time to prepare or reflect on ones actions.

Motivated Stalker – These are standard level stalkers, the amber level. They take care to plan, can appreciate skill and operate just within the boundaries of society. They see the endeavour as an art form to be perfected and upgraded wherever possible. They also have a further degree of control than opportunistic types. I consider myself to be at this level but with slightly more brain mapping than your average amber level.

Obsessed Stalker – Upper Register stalkers get into this category, red level deviants of the highest order. Stalk and kill is in this zone and anyone who goes in with human disregard, or with malicious intent. That's not playing the same game as everyone else and obviously misses the point of life generally I feel.

Casual Stalker – Aside from the above known stalkers, the casual type are the unknown novices that are higher in number, but lower in rating to all of the above. Mostly the occasional daydreamers but not actors, or who may have 'dabbled' a bit now and again but just remain an extra.

Creepy Stalker – These are the weirdo ones, the ones that follow and obsess but don't follow through or ever interact with their subject. I'm not sure they even realise their own motive, they may just be the one that think of themselves in disparaging terms which is what sets them apart from the others.

I personally think it's important to categorise behaviours and people, to understand the why and the how. To learn what people are and what they are capable of. They don't seem to take the time so I feel compelled to, to watch and learn, making assessments as I go. Some people make it to the 'Dr's Hall of Fame', it's the more interesting ones that I like to keep a record of. So I can remind myself of conclusions and revelations of the subjects that gave me the most. They all played their part in allowing me to be who I am today and I wish I could thank them. But that's my ego running away again, it's not an award, but self realisation and discovery can sometimes feel to the achiever that they have won an award. To have a break through of personality while giving someone a good hard fuck is an awesome feeling. Those are the keepers in my book.

I only met one other refined male predator actually like myself - I specify male as there is an influential female predator that later became an employer but that's another chapter. We crossed paths at a corporate seminar where I was always quite surprised at the apparent lack of sociopathic personalities. Those types of events actually brought out the submissive men who wanted to try and 'power up' their lives, but also brought out powerful women already taking control of theirs. My favourite. Because believe it or not; they are the ones who want to be dominated sexually the most in my experience. They have achieved a certain status of equality through competition in the workplace therefore the only competition left is in the bedroom. Women are as competitive and driven as men these days but all this does is up the stakes and opens the game to new possibilities. The extra bonus for me seems to be they have a slight belief they might win, that's what makes the game so much more fun.

But this seminar was different; I spotted a different look on one face when I scanned the crowd, the calculated nonchalance of a trained stalker. He looked about ten years senior to me and had the air of vastly more knowledge. How I thought I knew this is beyond me now but that's what my instinct said at the time. Naturally my ego and competitive traits had commandeered my instinct from that point as I had never come up against what I readily considered as competition. So I was pretty much doomed to miss the lesson. Youth and inexperience showed and didn't let me see the real beauty of this skilled stalker until I analysed the scene much later and a number of times. A lesson in being humble for my part it turns out as I missed the opportunity to learn so much more. Ego is an important part of everyone's mindset but for the predator it can overthrow or affect motive in a big way so I knew after that to be aware of arrogance and had to learn to keep it in check if I was to succeed in my intentions.

And for the record, my assumptions of superior skills were displayed when he procured my target right from under my nose. A flagrant show of mastery and elegance I had to admire later although couldn't fully appreciate for some years to come.

MY STALK & CATCH INTENTIONS

For me, there are two purposes to stalking, firstly for a means to an end and secondly for the act itself. I sometimes just like to watch, a rather interesting subject may come up whom although has no need of my full services directly, does require some attention. Fear is a very alluring aroma for me, but instability follows it around and that usually leads to trouble so be aware of the type of fear that attracts you and how to play with it.

I used my familiar ground and friends to build up a good knowledge of proximity, distance, judgement of times etc, mapping routes and detailing routines but not everyone is comfortable to overstep that personal boundary. I always felt I must be flexible in my goals and aspirations and have encountered variables at every turn especially once I am on unfamiliar ground. Being able to maintain an even more steady composure to complete your assignment becomes so much more important. If you are lucky enough to have already found that compliant partner then you have the chance to cut the stalking down to a minimum and take more time over the catch which after all, is the fun bit and a lot more interactive.

But as a general rule, try and not shit on your own doorstep. Apologies to say it so crudely but it is as it sounds. If you make it personal and select someone from your social group or workplace then you must be sure of no reprisals, this can be an easy stomping ground but also folly to whims and delicate personal politics you may directly be a part of. Exploiting unavailable women via this method is very acceptable though and surprisingly easy to get away with, one of those unspoken social standards you can take advantage of.

I pick my targets carefully and design my Stalk and Catch technique depending on my assessment of their requirement and level of denial. This can range from just needing a good fuck, to full on humiliation with all sorts in between. Putting all this together to make the assessment leads me to then having to put it all into action. I'm a doer after I'm a thinker. There are now extensive means of electronic monitoring which make my job a bit easier once I get to that stage, but you still can't escape from the old school follow and record routine. Knowing when someone leaves for work, knowing when they come home. How often do they go out in the evenings, do they live alone, are all key questions I ask myself and know before I pick a day to strike. If they don't live alone then I have to employ a slightly different set of rules but the game is still on, with extra care to really know I really won't be interrupted.

That's where I find planning to be my key to success, the stalk part is surprisingly easy; people don't take much care these days or notice the obvious when it's staring them in the face. It's the catch bit that can sometimes be tricky. The initial interaction and subduing is always a test of strength, speed and a fast smooth voice. Explain their situation, they're not idiots; inform them of what is happening calmly but extremely firmly. This is not a choice, this is an experience. Mostly I don't threaten their lives, unless highly hysterical, it's the only way to calm them enough without actually using heavy violence. That's not the kind of fear I'm after, I want looking at the door to see if they have time to run fear before they are caught. The kind of knowing fear I relish, not that an intruder is in their house, but seeing that they know they are not in control. Knowing they don't decide how this plays out. I don't like to hear the words, 'Take whatever you want' it seems so past the point. I want to hear 'What do you want me to do'. That would convey instantly they understand the situation they are in. I feel I may be asking too much with that one – but one can dream.

Although briefed above, this is but a small part of the catch. Once at the door or chosen location there is the case of identity. I have found it's rare to get through the front door unless you are following after a return out or know them but a balaclava usually does the trick until I have them blindfolded at least. Although depending on what you have in mind, sometimes fun to leave it on. Sort of like dressing up as a secret agent or terrorist and completing a mission of your own choosing. I'm good at sneaking up on them; it's such a rush, having gained entry through a window or unlocked door, from my previous watching I can usually tell the most effective way to get in. It's so exciting when they don't even know I'm in the house – again this goes back to stalking but an elevated level, in the house is red level stalking. Deciding on where to intercept can dictate how the whole situation can play out, it can be hard to predict where they are going to go in the house and if I wait too long run the risk of limiting my mission time. Self preservation is also of concern so I do try to not get lost in the moment too much. Often it will be a standard catch but the real gem is catching someone coming out of the bathroom already naked, it's priceless and rare, but does and can happen. It makes that moment of silence and hesitation from them so much more intense, the vulnerability much more exposed. No pun intended.

A hand grab to the mouth from behind is the usual method though and works. Being able to pull her in tightly against my chest; restricting movement with an arm and shoulder heavily bearing down, instantly winning the moment with a physical assertion of power. If there's too much distance it increases the probability of the fight or flight instinct kicking in, the real art in this situation is to stop this mechanism from happening altogether by taking away either of these options as available to her. A wilful subject may believe that a continued fight at this point is needed but soon realises this only ups the game for me and methods used to placate them.

I am a bit prone to being an outdoors kind of man for stalking and catching and have learnt to be precise with my assessments and timings. If I am following a subject home from a pub or supermarket for example, and do not intend to wait until she gets home, then timing and location is everything. If I have been skilled enough to get her to leave with me willingly then it will be different of course and I can decide easily, I have already caught her even if she doesn't know it yet.

I have also had the good fortune in the past to catch someone off guard completely; this doesn't require stalking per se, not much premeditated stalking anyway. This is opportunistic catching, seeing a moment, judging it quickly and then acting. This is more an ego boost I think for me; just to prove to myself that I can spot and utilise a moment in time without any pre conceived idea first of how it should play out. Actually a liberating feeling for someone driven by premeditation and planning like me, sort of stepping out of the comfort zone for a while.

I do not consider myself a lucky person, luck is a product of believing in fate and destiny, somehow rendering it out of your control. That's not for me;

luck is a matter of opinion or an excuse for not realising what has created a situation. That is not to say I cannot be swayed by a bit of fortune favours the bold ethos. There is much to be said for living in the moment or seizing an opportunity, but this just makes me observant, everything I planned previously or by going with the flow got me to that point. Therefore, I created the 'lucky' situation. I take credit for my work.

I try not to get disillusioned about what is going on when I have picked my target. I need to be careful not to reveal my hand to soon otherwise she will either detect a set up or it turns into a game in which she has control. Although it is tempting to either drop hints or try and engage in some kind of leading banter, I don't. She can, and I can listen and plan, but not return the gesture. Until I am ready to, probably more privately and planned through though. I have witnessed many a catch go astray because of this failure.

You may decide your workplace is the best arena for example and have had your eye on someone for some time anyway. Groundwork and laying the foundations are essential if you hope to pick up the correct subject. As I said previously, I don't stalk women that don't want to be stalked; they may just not know it yet. There are certain times when working late in the office has its advantages, especially if you are in control.

THE ART OF SUBMISSION

Once I have caught my subject, I need them to understand some basic rules in a rather short amount of time for one to be able to make good use of it. Compliance is paramount, safety is ensured and defiance will be punished. Keep it simple. This is where I find talking can help, don't give them time to think and make up their own judgement on where it's all going or it tends to freak them out. I give them instructions and even encouragement can be useful. It is important to be aware of stress levels throughout, mine and theirs for a satisfying encounter. Just because they aren't in control of what's happening doesn't mean they can't enjoy it. I always thought the thrill of a rollercoaster can be a similar ride; I know it's going to be scary and I can't stop it or get off once it's started. But I know where it goes and that it will stop, but that still doesn't stop me getting on and usually enjoying the ride.

The submission is ultimately about physical and mental control for me. Just pinning someone down isn't full control as it's just physical, and makes for difficult sex. Making them let you pin them down with minimal force is the trick. So they briefly believe they have some control by letting you fuck them. For some reason it seems easier for the mind to deal with by reacting like this rather than fighting back. It's what politicians and governments do to all of us all the time and we employ the same human tactic to take that shafting too.

Submission is not the same as compliance in my mind. Submission is to admit you do not have control and must come first; compliance is more understanding and comprehension of the situation and acting accordingly. I must sometimes override my subject's personal beliefs and expectation of themselves with my own agenda. They may have pre-disposed ideas of what they should do or not believe what I'm telling them. This adjustment doesn't usually take long if I'm consistent with my behaviour and do what I say. Quite often there has been compliance without submission, usually before I improved my knowledge of fear responses, but it can mean the lesson is missed for the subject. A review of previous material showed me where I was failing in my approach and led to a more rounded view for cause and effect.

I knew I needed to instil more confidence in my subjects to believe their own instinct and override their conditioning. Only then was I able to break down their emotional barriers, to strip away their very soul and make them mine to do with what I wanted.

I can honestly say I have saved marriages and destroyed relationships in equal measure through my studies but was merely the catalyst, not the actual cause. Denial is there behind all of them, rearing its ugly head to deceive and delay the inevitable and just prolong the torture that some people call life and marriage. To submit to your own yearnings first means you can move forward and help others with theirs, rather than hold each other in a doomed play.

THE PLACE OF DOMINANCE

I found it easy to make someone submit once I knew how, if the full submission fails then physical submission will always win and I still get a result. But to be able to correctly dominate the situation requires certain strength of character and the ability to think on ones feet. The building up of the dominant presence is a fairly standard one; it is easily achieved to all appearances and outward actions. But it is what happens behind closed doors that I found was the real test, to live the fantasy and carry out ones promises is not for everyone I'm sure. I can assure you though, this is not the type of role I could merely act, I had to live it and become my character for real, feeling the part as my own, presuming it had to be destiny it felt so comfortable. Making the previous years I have lived an act, it now felt like coming home to my own awareness I had put aside all those years ago.

What seemed to be most important was to not hesitate or show signs I am unsure. I can always buy myself some time by doing a body grip or pinning my subject against a wall, but this would highlight to me bad planning or lack of control. I'm not sure I can teach confidence but it is an important factor here, stalk and catch isn't for the faint hearted. Dominance extends into all areas of my life though, work, play, travel and hobbies. How someone views the opposite sex (or same sex if that's your preference), is crucial. As I said earlier, I respect women to talk to, to work with and to concede with over trivial matters, but when it comes to sexual matters I have to dominate them. To be able to dictate when, where and how gives me purpose and position that feels so unquestioningly normal that it must be. And women respond accordingly, further reaffirming this behavioural trait I have and do indulge in.

Weirdly enough though, I didn't like having a Dom/sub relationship, it was too premeditated (ironic I know), between the two parties. It felt like overkill submission to me and had so many rules and boundaries to discuss that it seemed more complicated than your average couple might have it. I just like the simple 'you're mine when I say' attitude. It has served me well too; just making it clear to women what I want while in certain establishments has worked in the past. I catch their eye but don't look away as they do. When they look back I'm still staring but then casually glance away as if there is such nonchalance about it that she is now interested. I stared for longer than a moment but wasn't then embarrassed, there's the show of confidence. And is what separates me from being a creepy stalker.

All evening though I don't make any effort to speak to her but keep up the regular checks on her to make sure no-one else has moved in to distract her. But equally, all evening she is deflecting any advances from potential entertainment and also keeping up regular checks on my position and if I am still checking. This is unspoken pulling, where the sexual telepathy happens and even though neither of you have spoken a word all night, you leave together – or at least within seconds of each other. Outside I lead her to my place if I've got the night free, or to the nearest alley if I'm feeling like an opportunist.

Still no talking sometimes, she knows what she left with me for, it's beyond implied and those are the unspoken rules. Sometimes there is confidence on both sides but it's still my job to take the lead, it used to be confusing to my ego to have a confident energy bouncing back, also confusing to some doubters of dominance to have women at this point show any signs of hesitation. Any drop in confidence can shake theirs that I will take charge and maintain control. But I push through any doubts and replace it with desire, very quickly remembering the purpose of my intent and with it focus and creativity.

AM I IN CONTROL

Self-control is paramount in all my studies, as well as being able to control your subject, unforeseen circumstances and the outcome. Life is open to variables so again, thinking on your feet is essential and being flexible is important. If I get too fixed on a goal I am likely to miss important alarm bells, potential opportunities or worse still, make a very bad judgement and end up incarcerated.

I didn't lack control as a child or young adult, I just craved it where I knew I could have it. I've never had a problem with authority figures or the establishment because I understood how it all worked and how to work within it. That doesn't mean I think its right, I just know what to say and do to have an easy life and not rock the boat, too much. Life would be no fun without a little wayward thinking and you must stand up for what you believe but only when the time is right.

But there is an undeniable system of control we live in, it would be ridiculous of anyone to pretend otherwise, but I know they do. They like to believe the system would only want to control us for our own good; it's for our safety and our future. It is not. The controller is interested in keeping control, by whatever means necessary usually, but will always prefer subtle, not too radical, quiet change that will slowly take you piece by piece so you won't notice until it is too late. There won't be enough pieces left to fight back with. It's a drawn out knowing fear tactic that has been used for generations past and takes a while, but still we sleep through it and continue to let it unfold.

We are the proverbial frogs in hot water. We didn't notice when they dropped us in cold water, we didn't even feel it when it started to heat up and now we are stuck in a personal dilemma. Do we 'wake up' and jump out, meaning we have to think for ourselves, trust our instincts and our friends and fight for our future? Or do we wait, hoping they will turn it down again, fearing to jump, fearing to wake. Still denying what it is? Only time can answer that one, I don't usually afford hope to much in my life, but I do hope for society to free themselves or at least to feel when the time has come to wake up and act.

Control is a funny illusion; we believe we are consciously in control of our own actions and thoughts every day, but in reality we are just following a set of pre-disposed rules and ideals set upon us from the word go. Handed down to us through generation and tradition; reconfirmed at every turn of our waking lives, except from deep inside our soul. We subconsciously suppress our desires and instincts so that we can consciously follow the system of control that is society. That is how things are; I am fine with this because I can't change it. But once you are aware of it, aware that you are different from the ordinary drone and that someone else controls your life, something has to be done to reintegrate yourself into this society that you are already a part of if you want to survive within it.

I merely take advantage of those who have not yet woken up and assist those who need help to step from the shadows to realise there is an alternate reality alongside the one you think you know. Running parallel to the normal order of how things appear to be, and running quite smoothly alongside it I might add. Corruption and control are what run this and every country around the world, every corporation, every life. All we have left is what we are and want to become, take control of your own life and the rest will follow.

I believe control is purely based on beliefs and perspective. If I make my subject believe that I am controlling them, then I have total control. If they think I do not control the situation for any reason then it gives rise to unpredictable behaviour, confusion on their part as to what their reaction should be and irrational actions can follow. The perspective part is down to the subject and is rarely changeable compared to beliefs strangely enough. It's hard for people to view their own life situations while going through them.

It is a fine balance to live in such a constructed fantasy when it finds such a fitting place in

'reality'. I know deep down that I don't really control anything, but that is what makes it so much more fun for the moments I appear to. I play my part so well; I just have very untrained counterparts to work with who need direction and guidance. I admit, I have lost a few days when indulging in extremes and have had to take a few days more after to return to my version of normal.
Counselling myself of the new plague of ideas and games I want to try. Input leads to creative output for me; I just have a different view of the word creative than most. But unless you control your urges, desires and instincts with logic and reason you can't hope to attain fulfilment and are left with that empty void of hate that will eat you alive and consume you in the darkness of yourself.

There is also matter of greed that must be touched upon within control. It can creep in and overshadow control so insidiously that I almost didn't notice how it became my motive. It's tricky and persuasive so be warned. Just because I want a piece, doesn't mean I have to eat the whole pie. Don't let greed push you beyond your better instincts but don't deny yourself either if that was your objective.

Many people don't understand greed though; it's like a subconscious want, out of control that latches onto your reward and pleasure centres. Feeding what feels like an uncontrollable urge to do whatever it wants and everything else can go to hell. Self-control <u>must</u> override greed. To have that feeling of power over your own desires can be very stimulating for someone of my disposition, and only then can I expect to harness someone else's.

For any society to work there must be a reasonable attitude within it and a fairly standard idea of what reasonable is. When societies grow together the boundaries are learnt and compromise can be achieved. But that is not how man has evolved. Instead there are personal agenda's instead of a prime directive, which loses sight of what is important or right for all. Because all don't know what is right? Who decides who is right, who can be the arbitrator for everyone? Personal accountability is everything and self-denial will do everything it can to avoid this but you must understand, we are all accountable. Don't hide from it, judge yourself. I do this on a routinely basis if not daily. I question my motives and objectives and re-evaluate them to make sure, I only retain control by being aware of it and maintaining it. Life is a work in progress and mine is no different, constantly throwing new challenges and situations to understand and learn from. I wouldn't want it any other way.

THE FACE OF FEAR & DEAL OF PUNISHMENT

I adore fear. The very thought of it, what triggers it, how it manifests, what it makes people do, where it can take you and how it can hold you back. Fear inspires me to control it, whether it is mine or someone else's. It took me a while to understand it and what it can make you capable of and in the right circumstances and applied in the correct doses it can achieve marvellous results for the studier. It has been through much trial and error I have found this out with some emotional damage left in its wake. Not on my side of course, I deciphered the meaning of events and assimilated it into my ways, adapting where necessary. But I felt it was important to know my limits and how to push them but at the same time not to miss the relevance of it all.

My favourite type of fear is a knowing fear that has a building period. To make someone not feel threatened or under observation is the trick. It won't be until later that they realise this mistake, when there is no-one else left in the room but them and I. And still there is no danger, I haven't created it yet. But as soon as I do, the atmosphere changes and becomes electric. It triggers her proximity alert and she is now sensing something, she glances up and then quickly away, I'm not any closer but she can feel me looking now. An uneasy shifting of the chair and the realisation slowly dawning on her, but still not accepting the instinctual warning signs of fear. Denial can be beautiful to watch. Seeing the internal trauma of unnaturally suppressing a natural reaction to fit in with how the world is expected to be rather than viewing the world how it is. Predicting how people will react is my forte and my favourite, a very rewarding feeling when I am proven right and a great learning curve when I am not.

There are quite a few different types of fear in my experience so I have tried to categorise them as best I can to hopefully explain what it is I am learning from my subjects.

Pre-Fear – this tends to be known as apprehension in normal circles, but I see it as pre fear, the type that leads to the outcome of real fear if I control it correctly. Sometimes I can control the situation but don't dictate it. Things happen that I can't control, but that doesn't mean I can't try my best to control things that do happen.

Fear Fear – this I see as a terrified fear of not knowing if their life is in danger (That kind of fear I find slightly cruel but like just a little now and again I can't help myself). It makes people react in very extreme ways and can severely impede an experience. It also makes control very difficult and subdue/submission near on impossible. I suggest to others to avoid at all costs unless you are very adept at dealing with it.

Knowing Fear – (Also known as building fear and follows on from pre-fear) when they are trapped but don't know it straight away. This type is fighting against their natural instincts telling them there is danger but they don't quite recognise it or believe it's real. This is my favourite I must admit, their confusion builds as do my intentions, culminating usually in a game where I win. Who wouldn't love that?

Compliance Fear - they comply but because they are scared I may be lying about not hurting them. Assuming I have verbally communicated this of course to avoid fear fear, but it is still only one step from it away so I tread with caution and watch out for warnings with this one. I want them to be submissive but not too scared.

Self-Judging Fear - When they realise they have made a mistake leaving with me and judge themselves for it. This is the easiest type to work with, once someone has left with me after spending time during the evening it's a win. It is implied and once you get them to the desired location, they don't really have a say. This type of pull is more for the domination side rather than stalking obviously but I never know when it will dawn on them. I have to take charge on the journey, be forceful and presumptuous. Judgement fear tends to lead to knowing fear very quickly, but has a difference, they blame themselves, and I can see on their faces, they know then that they let the wolf in. Let me make this clear at this point, this is not flirting. I am controlling the fear situations I have created; I have targeted someone and am making them feel targeted but not entirely threatened until I want them to, ideally when they are trapped. In the pursuit of fear and control I will always use the threat of and action of punishment if necessary. I find it can be used for a range of controls, pleasures and dominance related activities depending on the subject and purpose of my experiment or activity.

Punishment also covers a range of things I use to make them submissive depending on their will and pleasure. It ranges from flogging and spanking to mild torture or extreme if that's the requirement with much in between. I also use it to enhance an experience; not just for disobedience, they don't need to know it's coming, only I do. I'm in control.

Threat of punishment – This would be for achieving submissive behaviour, but must be followed through if challenged. I always know in advance what I am going to use. I don't need to tell them, they only know the word punish, it can be whatever I want.

Possessive Punishment – How I deliver my punishment is important, it's a possessive punishment I'm giving and she has disobeyed knowing the consequences will be my disapproval. And my disapproval leads to punishment, it's all very simple.

Aggressive Punishment – Some people with anger issues struggle with this one, I never dish out retribution in anger, as I run the risk of losing control – of myself and of my subject.

I do have a liking for sadistic acts in control situations though, seeing how far I can push someone and watching the enjoyment and barriers being worked through. It gives me that feeling of adrenaline I crave so much, so punishment and pain is another personal favourite in my studies. And I would be lying if I said I didn't enjoy the power too, to own someone completely for that time is very satisfying.

THE NATURE OF OBSESSION
& OBJECT OF DESIRE

I define an obsession as something that consumes you, mind body and soul. It impedes your ability to think properly, sleep, eat, you are not happy unless you know you can achieve the task of feeding it. It takes you. If it fits the above described all-encompassing feeling then it qualifies as worthy of attention and indeed may be an obsession. Otherwise you are probably fighting a losing battle if you should chose to try and ignore it as I did at first.

To be consumed by such a severe want or a lust is most distracting; it's almost like internal sabotage on a very personal level, feelings, memories, hormones and chemicals conspiring against you to drive what feels like an instinctual urge. Controlling or indulging the obsessions can be a full time job, maintaining a level of normality and yet being able to live with what drives you potentially round the bend. The only answer I found was to feed it and try to understand it as I thought I saw it at the time.

I understood from fairly early on that obsessions developed if I wasn't able to do what I felt I had to. I would think back to a time before the new subject had taken over my life, to what drove me then and why it hadn't felt so intense. It was because frustration wasn't allowed to build up inside and help to create the obsession, because I allowed it to it run its course and either let it go naturally or integrate the new subject into my life. All children are prone to obsession and fascinations that can extend into adulthood. How they are treated by your parents is usually the determining factor of which way they go. Obsessions can quickly turn into disorders if not kept in check, the unfortunate ones who are not able to work through this self-created mental system; end up working through the government imposed mental system instead, or spending a lifetime in therapy and denial. Application of intelligence goes a long way sometimes to save oneself. If you can look at yourself and be your own judge of character then it helps. Also keeping the need for external intervention to a minimum so as to live one's life as undisturbed but as fulfilled as possible while engaging in obsessive activities of any kind.

The obsession of domination however, and the one that took me so completely, could rarely be satisfied I found. There are so many areas that can be explored that it makes it too difficult to ever really feel like you can close a chapter and move on. My downfall is always wanting to go back and re-run the experiment because as time goes on my mindset changes or I have adapted my way of thinking about things and feel I would benefit from a new experience within an old formula. It can get overwhelming and time consuming to be this way but I couldn't change this if I wanted to. This is why sharing the obsession can help, to a point; it's difficult to believe anyone can truly understand your nature unless they also harbour deviant tendencies. It is a quite an unburdening feeling though to be able to freely talk about desires most dark.

It's thought that obsession is down to choice. People think they have choices, to believe that you are in control of your own destiny, fate and desire. This is not the case in my opinion. Darker still is that the illusion of choice is as it sounds, an illusion and choice doesn't even exist. There is only manipulated free will constructed to appear as such in order for the mind to cope with such an instinctual demand that has been placed upon it within modern living. I feel I can take advantage of this loophole in society and can use the manipulated for my own studies, even if that means assisting them to wake up and understand their own life and desires along the way.

Within the objective of desire there must always be a muse. It's important as I said before to have a target and goal, to have purpose and point makes one's life a more enriching experience. Whatever the purpose or point may be, as long as it means something to you then it is worth it. My purpose is to study people, to watch and know about what makes us all tick and pushes us to the very edge of ourselves and sometimes beyond. I just happen to have a 'quirk' in my programming that makes me like to deviate from the 'norm', but actually has given me more access to what I am purposed to do. So am I actually a deviant in the conventional sense of the word or am I just human?

My object of desire and obsession is and has always been knowledge. About myself firstly as no-one can really know you like you – once you strip away the self-denial and years of conditioning of course. But then to see what's out there, to really see what I see made it impossible not to be driven by a need to understand. Every day to leave your house and be presented constantly with confidence, fear, joy, worry, happiness and sadness can be thoroughly overwhelming and draining unless you can either shield yourself from it, or be prepared to take it all in and analyse it. The ability to process and understand all of these emotions we are all bombarded with internally and externally does not mean I have to be afflicted by them. Quite the contrary, I find it increases my awareness of what triggers them and find it easier to avoid falling into the same trap as others around me. But after all, being human will still make you prone to mistakes from time to time. This is not a defeat and should never be taken as so, this is learning.

It's important not to lose sight of your life or those in it in pursuit of indulging a whim, desire or obsession. I don't only stalk or I will lose the ability to communicate effectively, jeopardise my current situation or just plain slip into creepy stalker mode and end up one of societies rejects. Be it not better to take part and indulge in society rather than skirt around the edges? Fun and hedonism are too frowned upon these days, but in the pursuit of ourselves are we not allowed to enjoy nature's bounty?

MY UNINTENTIONAL KILL

It's as it sounds. The worst mistake of my life was an incident that occurred just after college before I entered the work world for my real adult life of servitude. I hate to trivialise it by calling it an incident, it was a disaster, I'll call it what it was and although deeply shamed and I find it regrettable I can't say I afforded much guilt to this action, although I have toiled with whether I should have or not.

She was slightly too keen to experiment and I was slightly too keen to push her and my limits and boundaries all in one go. Adolescent hormones still tormented me (and possibly still do to this day), and I felt like I couldn't do everything fast enough. We met and seemed to have that unspoken sexual telepathy going on and didn't need to openly flirt or even talk to get each other's attention. We met unseen and away from anyone we knew and delighted in exploring what we had only fantasised about.

We tried some moderately tame bondage at various outdoor locations, we would sort of play early cat and mouse in the woods, me stalking her and catching from behind, tying her to a tree or just going for the direct approach which was quite developed by now. Many a fun time were had in those woods and surrounding fields, once or twice nearly being caught by dog walkers just adding to the excitement of it all for both of us and possibly the dog walker, I wasn't really aware of the other types of woods based sexual activities at that time that any number of adults partook in.

But it was different though on this occasion. It felt quite dark in the woods that day; I sensed it as we walked in and I felt a shudder down my spine, an oppressive heaviness that could have been mistaken for evening mist, but I could feel it. It gave me a new feeling of jaded control and power I hadn't experienced before and suppose looking back now know that it was I that entered the woods with that feeling changing the way I saw things. But at the time I tried to convince myself that I alone was surely not capable of that type of cold hearted villainy. That I must have been influenced by some dark force that had commanded a sacrifice and I willingly obliged. Taking on something else in place of my own personality and resulting in a moment of insanity. If only I could have hidden behind that.

I had only been liaising with this girl for about two weeks and we were only on first name terms, I knew she had a boyfriend though so all the sneaking around suited her just fine. I thought I was showing imitative by taking one of my father's ties along, thinking I could gag her or use it for further restraint, in my mind later I believed adding to what seemed like premeditation on my part. She hadn't minded handcuffs in the past but had very clearly shown reluctance to anything else.

This is where my inexperience showed and I thought I knew better, and I still believe I did, but just applied it incorrectly. Once I had her half naked and handcuffed beneath me, the weight of my body straddling hers, the feeling of power was now completely overwhelming for me and I pulled out the tie and I put it around her mouth; she instantly got a fear fear look on her face. In future this is the look that makes me judge my reactions very carefully and handle things properly, at this time I did not possess that insight. Instead choosing to assert a strange and possibly not entirely my own dominant feeling over her, I wanted her to comply, to know I could do whatever I wanted and suddenly employed violence to achieve it. I moved the tie from around her mouth and slipped it down to her neck. Her naked legs were starting to try and kick behind me and cuffed hands did their best to try and fight me off, but I just thought I could do it for a few moments and she would understand that I was in control and stop fighting me. But she didn't stop, so I didn't stop. I felt like we were in a battle of wills over who would concede and I had to be the victor, at all costs it seemed. It didn't feel like a good win.

There was no joy or relief, only sadness and sudden clarity of mind that could have knocked me over with a feather. Not even a flutter of excitement resounded through me; this had overstepped one of my few personal boundaries and rendered me so completely out of control. I couldn't change this, make it better or affect the result now in any way. This type of activity it turned out, what not for me at all. I had obviously played briefly with the idea of killing as a past time, wondered if I was indeed that depraved to want human suffering, but felt it was too final and counterproductive on society and self-learning. I wanted people to live, learn and experience, not to experience and die without years ahead for reflection, I had worked out mentally and morally that it was against what I stood for. I didn't need to know how it felt, but know how it feels I do. And the loss of control leading up to it too, it was the stark opposite of what I wanted and I have never experienced it again like that to this day.

But it did give me a new insight into the consequences of uncontrolled play as well as how the mind can work when it finds itself perpetrating that kind of act under the believed circumstance of unintentional. I still don't know what it must be like to carry around that kind of malice of forethought with you so consistently that you are driven to feed it and indulge it, although I understand obsession so maybe I'm not as far away from the underlying force as I would like to think.

I removed her remaining clothes and pocketed the tie and cuffs for cleaning; we were in quite a dense part of the woods so there is where I buried her. I dug the pit with my hands and a stick, feeling the cold earth in my hands matching the stare from the body. Luckily the time of year and rainfall meant loose earth underfoot and under hand but I still dug my hand in deep, dragging my fingers over the mud as I pulled and scrapped. I felt so angry at myself and at the mercy of the whims of the world, at what I had done and how I couldn't go back, I had changed forever. It felt cathartic to grab at the earth and feel a connection to life while in the morbid company of death, a slight soothing to my suddenly tormented soul.

Still, the longer I spent in the corpses company it made it hard to separate myself from the act which led us here. However much I had already tried to justify it to myself, I couldn't while she was there, next to me still. But I knew I had to feel this, remorse had a purpose and I was on the receiving end of this harsh self-imposed lesson.
I turned her over to face me, so I could really look at what I had done and take in the cold hard fact; I let her cold blue eyes look through me. To make myself get it, the gravity of it, the reality of it, the life changing shock of it. This was real, I had to accept that and not bury the memory and lessons as I was going to bury her. To waste this tragically beautiful moment would be itself another disaster.

And it was over; I finished my self-inflicted grim task and walked away with only time and this

memory to now follow me forever. But I do tend to stay away from the woods at night though if in company, not entirely for my sake of course.
.

INCARCERATION

This is prison to the layperson, and every measure should be undertaken to avoid for your own self-preservation, but the act can be utilised and incorporated into your repertoire of situations and scenes. I take time to choose my target carefully and understand their requirements and not to let my imagination run too riot. I have spent a certain amount of time within the confined walls of various prisons, for a time early in my career I was employed by the system to study, comment and evaluate incarcerated folk and have managed to learn a great deal from these years and experiences.

I had naively assumed that to find these men in a prison would surely mean they would be of inferior intelligence or somehow less deviant and less cunning than me, and for some that was certainly the case. But there were a few that seemed capable of the same level of precision and planning as me. Who had charm, wit and were educated but just seemed to have what others considered 'bad luck', this was a lesson in humility for me. To realise even some of the best can be caught out occasionally made me take more caution over my endeavours and not let arrogance guide me as it seemed to have them.

I found the study of prisoners fascinating though, as interesting as people on the outside in 'free' society but obviously affected massively by the gender specific inhabitants and their general attitudes and reason for being part of this segregated lifestyle. But strangely I found that the prison attitude was carried out into what we called normal society and communities. A feeling of being trapped with no hopes for a future, a disdain of daily life although being afforded all the freedoms that are so denied while being behind locked gates, I never understood how this transfer was so seamless and I still wonder it now and again to this day.

Back to the main point of including this act in my research; a careful board to tread, incarcerating someone is a very delicate operation and takes planning. This easily can turn into kidnapping so there is a need to create some rules first and know the person won't be missed for the length of time I have in mind. It's quite a turn on to go out and do my shopping knowing there is a tasty morsel at home waiting where I left her, ropes and all. But I don't let this power go to my head; power and control can be a dangerous combination if unbalanced, I knew I must understand my intentions on where I wanted it to go and why.

A particular favourite expedition of mine will give you a more comprehensive view of my procedure and insights into how the scene unfolds.

She was a friend of mine's girlfriend and weirdly enough it was he who gave me the Intel needed so I didn't even have to stalk really, such simple words to prick my attention; he was going away for the weekend. Now, I said I can spot a predatory male from a mile away, but most men seem to completely lack this radar. Preferring to rose tint the world as per conditioning and upbringing, rather than feel what should be felt. His mistake is my good fortune. But more than just mention his trip, he then continued to talk, firstly about how his girlfriend would be stuck at home all weekend studying for some exam and had shunned the world for this time. I took it all in, letting my mind log and work through all the information he was giving me. He then went onto to then cover his weekend's plans and movements with even an estimated time of return.

He had no idea what I had started planning straight away. Only once have ever I sensed a setup, people have give away signs when they are hiding something or lying, there is just something not logical in their reasoning which makes me question their motive. But for this instance, there were no alarm bells, I was good to go. I had met her on a number of occasions and she had already been coveted I must admit, like I said before, I had a special fancy for already claimed women. But I knew the rules and would never have shit on my own doorstep if not been invited to as such. Anyone else may have just taken his information and thought no more of it, but that's the difference between they and I.

I don't have to actively analyse things, more try to not if anything. They just fall into logical place mostly and I have a 'holding cell' for unresolved theories or new ideas to be tested and turned into theories to prove. I had decided through my observations that she could be swayed and coerced and ultimately end up blaming herself, a win win for me. There is a weakness of character that is so easy to manipulate. I find the concept of manipulation wonderful and simple. It is often used out of context and is feared because people think it represents a subconscious lack of control. It is merely to take advantage of what one sees to get what one wants. If the other person is not entirely aware of your tactics then why should it bother them? As soon as they comprehend manipulation, they feel justified in feeling hard done by. I can see why they do based on their reasoning but I still don't fully understand this reaction, it's not logical.

But I wander, I will return to the story in hand. So, it's Friday night, he's away, she's alone. A few status updates confirm the plan is still the same, night in alone with study books, signing off until Monday. I thought through all the different types of approach but chose the very bold and not often used knock on the front door without hiding your identity. You have to know the person for this to even remotely work and you have to get in quick, whether it be pretending to need the toilet or just talking your way in, you decide at the time. You should also have assessed from her reaction and how she is holding the door, if you are in or have to work for your meal.

There will be a number of clear emotions from such an up close and personal interaction. Because at this point she still thinks she decides if you are coming or not, and every man knows there is just a slight moment when you are alone with a female (not related ones of course), that unspoken hesitative awareness of vulnerability and possible plundering that could take place. This one was confusion as to why I was at the front door but not guarded enough or aware as the door was being held open in an unspoken invitation way.

This was politeness at its best and most productive. Many mistakes of virtue and vice have been made out of politeness; it can also be a massive contributing factor to self denial. I will therefore always use to my advantage if I can. Hers was working overtime here, not only invited in, but seated and given a beverage. Half the work has been done for me, but that doesn't take away any of the fun, I get to apply some knowing fear and watch from a spectacular view point as it unfolds. She can feel some tension in the room as she returns with my drink and it's because I am creating it. Something between sexual tension and stalk your prey intimidation that is intriguing and beguiling.

Again it's about energy here, a poker face serves me well and I can make someone feel watched without showing it on my face. The darker of the watchers will have worked this out already and be aware of 'tone of emotion' in facial expressions you make and see, but most women don't. It's as she places my drink and starts to retreat I strike, grabbing her wrist and standing quickly to give me the upper hand in the capture. Surprise for a fleeting moment, that stand still moment I look forward too, of excitement and anticipation. But then a new look, submission and knowing seeping in, she's a sheep and she let the wolf in. Although if you think about it we were already in, they just didn't know it.

Through her actions alone I judged her as compliant. I was allowed to pander to every whim I had without much protest, to experiment as I saw fit and observe and enjoy the results. I did not break her, that was not the goal. I did push her though, to and through a limit she didn't even know she had, putting a new set of beliefs about herself in motion and giving me an astounding sense of achievement. I 'released' her from my service on Sunday afternoon and went about my business, she failed her exam but didn't seem too disappointed with the result overall. Instead finding her way very quickly into a full on D/s relationship with someone new. Strange how little people know about themselves when it comes down to it.

Many people are stuck in their own private prisons in their mind or society, I feel I help them to realise what is hidden or being suppressed. Of course I have my own selfish motivation for assisting in their need; I am not deluded about my real purpose for being there. But knowing you can bring change to someone who is at a tipping point in their lives brings out the professional in me; I put on my best suit and go to work.

MY LOVE OF GAMES

One of my interests (and possibly obsessions) is games. There are a number of opportunities that can be used to initiate a game or two while out and about or if just having a night in. The darker more premeditated ones require a more lengthy setting so I will explain some basic but not too time consuming possibilities. A range of techniques are usually employed within these games to achieve my goal.

Cat and Mouse – this requires a closed room ideally with some furniture, perfect for the office after hours or some of you may be lucky enough to have your own office like me. Ground work must be laid for this to be risk free. I find the scenario of standing behind the chair mentioned before becomes important in this setting; an amateur may think a move to be next to their subject will increase the intensity of the situation but this just shows a lack of control and overview. By standing behind, I can easily elevate the level the knowing fear without having to act rashly. Hands on the shoulders at this point is usually a good start, that way I get instant skin contact, but I can also feel her muscles tense. That initial thrill is mesmerising, applying slight pressure to make sure she knows to stay put, I can feel the triggers which makes her want to stand but I override them.

Slightly massaging her neck and shoulders isn't enough though at this stage, leaves room to misinterpret my intentions, so I move my hands down and start to unbutton her blouse. This is where I get a reaction, sometimes compliance and no fear or real fun in my opinion (you can still get some without a struggle sometimes), or let them try and escape. This gives me the chance to follow them to the failed exit point and coerce away. Pin them, tease them about letting them go, go straight in, whatever you're creative mind can come up with at this point. Very gentlemanly of course in my mind, efficient and passionate, I enjoy what I do.

Direct Approach – Previously covered but want to bring in again to show how flexible it can be. It is easiest and most effective when my subject is horizontal but also achievable standing if there is something to push them against. Still good fun but often triggers the fight response. But the basic principle being to pin your catch and restrain with your speed and strength. It's a classic and easy way to render someone unequivocally captured though. At this point I can then employ handcuffs or a belt to tie their hands and limit their options.

Stalk and Catch - The principles of this are covered in the previous section but can be made to be as elaborate as I like. The only extra information I could possibly give would be to divulge one of my more memorable missions.

I had followed a woman back from the supermarket, I knew her house was empty and she would use the back door out of sight of the passing traffic. But I decided to already be in the house, I like it when I can hear them making their normal household noises when I am just waiting. Soon the inevitable footsteps up the stairs and she is so close now I'm sure she can hear my breath, my heart rate slows slightly as my strike time is near. My hand reaches out and clasps over her mouth from behind, forearm and elbow across the torso and I'm pulled in close behind her. Her whole body stiffens and the moment is held, I can feel her fear, this is just plain old fear fear as she still doesn't know what's going to happen yet. Is her life in danger? Am I a burglar? Am I a rapist? She struggles a bit now her mind is starting to work but I have her held effectively and it doesn't do much to thwart me. I'm still not saying anything because she isn't either, it seemed the right thing to do, but decide she has now lost that right anyway and use my other hand to pull a tape gag, blindfold and handcuffs from my back pocket. Good old trusted kit, in seconds she can't see, fight back or protest verbally.

I wanted to move her to the bedroom and had already removed some clothing but I couldn't resist seeing this half naked trussed up young women and wait any longer. Realising my mistake I removed her gag, told her not to say anything and just do as she was told. After instructed to be on her knees

and open her mouth, I unzipped my jeans and got the feeling I was looking for. Her lips closed around me as I entered her mouth and took my pleasure, seeing her down there at my mercy making it all the sweeter. Needing physical encouragement at this point I grabbed the back of her head to assist in the motion, to be sure she understood her role in this play. It was so engrossing I found it hard to keep my mind on the schedule. I needed to move on.
Half being dragged and half stumbling, she was led to the bedroom and I closed the door. She started to try and back away towards the far corner of the room creating an unforeseen game of cat and mouse that just added to this already incredible experience. She hadn't tried to remove the blindfold so couldn't even see where I was in the room and had no idea this was just getting me hotter. Enough was enough; she was going to get it. Lifting her by her cuffed wrists I chucked her roughly on the bed and started to undo my belt. She didn't try getting away this time, the belt seems to have a very powerful effect even when just heard, renders them powerless, they know what you are taking it off for and it doubles as an incentive against defiance.

I pulled her towards me and bent over the edge of the bed; her half open shirt exposed perfect breasts and only had a pair of small white lace panties on. I pulled these down slowly and snaked my hands down her back, moving over her buttocks and down further. I pushed two fingers into her and felt my own urge stiffen; she was already damp and ready for it. But her slight moan served only as incentive for me to stop playing so nice, I withdrew my fingers and plunged myself into her deeply, slightly lifting her feet off the floor to do so. I found my rhythm and did my worst. I tend to lose track of time a little bit while enjoying the final scene, before the curtain falls and its back to 'reality'.

Control went out the window on this one and I really went to town. I am not usually one to precisely kiss and tell but I understand that my readers may have wanted slightly more than just suggestion of events and may have required some detail, so in the interest of politeness I have obliged to a point. We are discussing the art of stalking and deviant sexual behaviour, not how to have sex.

Alone in the House - This is the game everyone can play; it covers stalkers, lovers, married and anyone who wants to engage in the role-play of stalk and catch. Sneaking into your own house has its merits, especially if the person in there doesn't know your going to do it. To leave them deliberately abandoned in their hour of need, not quite knowing if you are someone else or in fact who they think it is. I always leave a window unlocked and wait until she has gone for a shower, then you get the rare treat of no obstructions on your mission to debase her.

Standing in from of the closed bathroom door, I wait, trying to imagine the type of fear that her face will betray her with before her brain can think properly. It opens, ah, delight, its fear fear. But only for an instant because the knowing fear creeps over her quickly. But still slight confusion, it was not mentioned when or where I might strike so it could still be a stranger, no talking definitely helps to keep the fear up and the balaclava keeping me anonymous for now. But she still wonders. Is this the one I arranged and am I safe? Or is it one I didn't arrange and I should be reacting differently? That type of study is psychology gold and is hard to find and execute effectively.

I know I've got her and can make her think whatever I want, treating her quite roughly gives the doubts room to grow and also gives you the chance to show your dominance and control of the situation and her. It may sound funny but if you have to talk, then make it short commands. I don't want to spoil the game and give her too much power. Some women mistakenly think that by agreeing to a deviant liaison that they have any control over how far it goes. By agreeing to it you are waving a red rag to a bull and then trying to believe you can shoo it back into its enclosure and close the gates. Indeed this is not the case.

Having an en-suite bathroom proved to be a good choice and I easily manoeuvred her over to the bed. If anyone did happen to break into my house they would either find themselves luckily equipped as I did now, or would be very uneasy and probably leave rather quickly. The ornate looking leather handcuffs perfectly position in the upper centre of my headboard very quickly entrapping my catch. I decided a blindfold at this point would be prudent so I could discard the balaclava and properly enjoy the full uninterrupted view I had before me. If they know how to play the game they will ask you to stop and protest, not serving any purpose other than to make me want her more. The game is now afoot.

I find life would be quite a lot duller if I didn't have these instincts and urges to satisfy regularly, they drive me to succeed and move forward with my life, inspire me to seek out new limits and understand the inner mechanics of motive and desire.

Cloak & Dagger – It really should be called mask and knife but that doesn't have the same ring to it. I obviously wear the mask and have the knife initially, this I then give to my subject. Once armed they become quite a different catch (Cat and Mouse crosses over a bit here too), and it raises the level of intensity on both sides. She thinks she has a chance and I get to think of new strategies to both disarm and overpower. I guess it's the same as giving your prey a head start to make the hunt more exciting and sporting. I agree, it does. The knife never had any power and is only a superficial symbol, but people value symbols and give them more worth than they actually have. It's only the clever ones who know to drop the knife or not take it in the first place, the ones who had realised their predicament and know it's a set up. They are few and far between though and most will take the bait.

Hide and Seek – requires forethought and planning. Not available to everyone, but some of us are lucky enough to have a secure residence or friends with a lake side summer house. I have modified my house for such interactions making it incredibly easy to keep someone in, usually making their options basement or upstairs/attic. Any good horror fanatic knows they are the two rooms in the house where bad things happen to you so you would think they'd know. But predictability rears its head and my assumptions are correct. Either of these options will be starkly obvious as the wrong choice as soon as the awareness of surroundings kicks in for any subject though.

But it is up to you what games you may prefer, but imagination is always the key and stay focused, you can still learn while having fun.

D/s OR S&M?

I naturally found my way through my interests to the world of BDSM (Bondage, Dominance, Sadism & Masochism for those who are unfamiliar), and felt that a D/s situation might actually suit me (Dominance & submission). I figured I could be acceptably, but still secretly deviant this way and joined a group online and social networking sites to see what the general running order of arrangement would be. I met up with a girl after some preliminary talking and we tried for a couple of weeks but I was very put off by the initial contract arrangements about boundaries and limits that it took the fun away rather than shared it. That's part of the fun of discovery. I felt it actually made the unpredictability disappear rather than enhance it, part of what I liked the most. I didn't want her to know what I wanted to do; she required too many instructions and too much care. It felt like having a pet slave. Too submissive. I thought I needed someone who didn't know I was going to dominate them until it was too late.

S&M was definitely more to my taste though and the women who would partake of this exploration of the darker side of sex and pain fascinated me. It can also overlap into the realms of D/s easily as well but I liked that as it seemed to naturally occur under the circumstances and was not pre-set or organised. They are usually feistier too, putting up more of a fight on purpose to increase the threat of or dishing out of punishment. It's the perfect environment to learn to control your aggression, or not for some people, test some boundaries and indulge in some nicely dark adult consenting fun which leads to my favourite game within that realm. Not included in the games section, I felt this one needed to be set apart and in a better context as shouldn't necessarily be treated as a game.

Torture - Now this one will sting a bit, extreme, not for the faint hearted and MUST be with a consenting party. **Trust** will be a huge factor here, not covered much previously as it requires a submission of sorts up front from the subject, and probably won't be used much after this description. She knows there will pain, she doesn't know how this will be delivered, when, how much or when I will stop. That's about as up front as I like it to get. She only knows there will be no permanent scarring, ideally, and that I am in control. It's not good to go too far with the type of endeavour with someone who isn't of this ilk, so be careful not to start mixing your pleasures with someone who isn't.

But I enjoy punishing and inflicting the exquisite pain, to see the body flinch under my trashing strokes, to see the flesh begin to reveal it's sensations to the eye, gives me such a thrill. But to find the recipients pleasures and thresholds is quite the experience. To deem something punishable and delivering judgement and retribution as I see fit seems a natural consequence of being dominant and in control.

I have two well equipped rooms that I like to call my 'hobby rooms' but other more conventional terms could be dungeon and torture room. Although in the torture room I do have my writing desk and music collection so it is very much a hobby room for me. It's a very inspiring and creative place where good bad things happen. Patience is definitely a virtue in these types of hobbies as with any, but the rewards can be just. Knowing when to wait is part of the game, and one must always play wisely with decorum and finesse.

Learning about timing will naturally lead you to understand more about patience and most of you will know if you have it or not. It's much easier to detect and admit than other qualities I've discussed and mentioned, but should be an easy one to grasp. The point of it is to be able to know when to use it, there is no time limit on your excursions, except the ones you place upon it depending on your assessments or goals.

If you are just looking to get your end away, cheat on your wife or just stalk and catch any subject and make them into a victim then you have missed the point and will probably miss the lesson in people too. It's about being able to observe and understand human instinct, something that I find is very hard to teach but I am giving it a shot in basic form. Reading my opponent, prey, competition, adversary or whatever my fight is against or observation is of is paramount in achieving control of the situation and being able to affect the final result.

MY EQUAL AND CONFIDANT

I was extremely lucky to meet the most influential woman in my life to date. An exploitative mistress to rival the best devious mind and soul I had ever thought I could be or would ever hope to meet. Up until this point I suppose I had led quite the lonely existence, just accepting that I was set apart from the average person, mentally and intellectually but I never had really considered the emotional differences I displayed. It does sound very short sighted on my part I know.

I found her during a stalk and catch operation ironically enough; I guess that's how someone like me would be destined to meet someone like her. It was a couple of days into my monitoring schedule when I noticed that she was watching me too, I had been spotted but she was playing the game. This was a turn up for my books, I had never had to react to this before and it changed the objective slightly as I had obviously miscalculated somewhere along the line her need or requirement. But I went with it and continued to follow and watch. And she continued to let me. I wondered if she knew where it would go, got that familiar feeling of control and even though I was in self denial about who was really in control here, it felt right.

I think for one of the few times in my life I actually romanticised this situation. I forgot we weren't flirting and I broke my own rules. At least it was with her though, no harm, no foul. I picked my afternoon having noted there was no real activity or visitors during the day and she appeared to live alone; another real lesson for me in humility, just because people go in doesn't mean they have left by the next day. I saw her go into the house leaving the back door slightly ajar. I took the bait and followed, making my way to the back door and gently closing it as I entered. It was quite a closed space for how the house looked on the outside, like it should be spacious and light, not dark and looming as this was. I liked it though, made me feel at home.

I couldn't tell which way she had gone so decided hide and seek would be fine, not knowing the layout of the location can make it even more exciting, or scary depending on which side of the fence you stand. But where I stood, is on the brink of a once in a lifetime opportunity. I could now hear something up the stairs and took my lead to investigate, I am never armed in these situations (unless you plan some cloak and dagger), as it gives rise to options that aren't necessary. A door is slightly open and I follow like a moth entrapped in the mesmerising light ahead, not quite able to see in the room but I can tell someone is in there. Someone, but not who I am stalking! Instead I find another woman, already through stage one of capture, cuffed, blindfolded and already showing signs of fear fear. You may feel that someone else putting in the work could feel like a defeat, never, it's just a variable to think spontaneously about and act accordingly; good fortune is not something to turn your nose up at.

Taking half the task away gave me more time to indulge in what I enjoy the most. Inflicting the right doses of pleasure and pain and to have unwavering control over your subject and actually have them begging for more rather than to stop. Strangely, the not knowing enhanced my interest in her, I didn't know who she was, who she belonged to if anyone or why she was here. Potentially she didn't know any of these things either, another pawn in the trade of people perhaps. It did take away some of the restrictions I usually placed on myself I must admit, I allowed my control to go further and test itself. I presume this is where I may have left some real emotional damage in my wake; a tainted, empty and downright abused individual was what I left behind. But I am still human and can also be taken by the darkness a bit every now and then.

When I returned downstairs, my original goal was sat at her kitchen table, with a coffee and cigarette in hand looking quite smug with herself. I looked at her, I mean really looked this time, not with the same eyes that had been stalking her for the last few days. At the tight wrap around dress that clung to her, that fell elegantly over her exposed creamy thighs, very tight and revealing. Great dark hair, well kempt generally and a look I had not seen before on a woman. A darkness of mind that was no longer hiding, or pretending to be vulnerable, she sat there for what she was. A predator. A dominator like me, someone else accepting their differences and exploring them. It was most odd to see that look on a woman, what I usually viewed as my subjects and prey, was suddenly my equal. A range of emotions and thoughts then followed. I hadn't really ever considered a predatory female before, not without a man behind them at least, so firstly I was faced with an actual feeling of helplessness, and to know she sought what I did meant I wouldn't ever get it from her.

That I supposed was only natural for someone who subjectified woman as I did but I don't ever recall that feeling when I knew a man was like that. She admitted she had watched me accept her gift, and that she really did like to watch in all manner of ways. We sat and talked instantly at ease in each other's company. It actually felt good to hear someone else talk of what I had kept hidden for so many years, to be so free about what they wanted. She turned out to have quite a different set of motives than I did though, as well as a number of deep seated issues and underlying personality disorders but this just added to the wonder I felt.

Part of her interest lay in why women could get away with a whole lot more than men although we claimed to be living in a more equal world. She felt women took advantage of this but only when it suited them. Although she was a dominator, very easily she would use submissive tactics if necessary. She liked to wind men up to turn them into a dominator, then dominate the fuck out of them, it really messed with their heads but she loved it and it caused the element of danger I assumed she was looking for. And I had not had the chance for this kind of study before and was hooked instantly, it gave my mind so much to work with and such a feeling of excitement I was doomed from the start.

How she became my employer was through a venture she had had underway for a while, and needed someone like me for the head job. As it's not the kind of role you can interview for and it had taken a while to find me but there would no shortage of 'work'. Then she elevated herself again in my books to tell me of her business, that she had a number of clients and associates that place orders for premeditated 'rape'.

I was sceptical of course, again, it sounded too good to be true, but it was true. Good money changed hands for the arrangement for husbands, wives and disgruntled enemies to exact revenge or just indulge a fantasy for someone. I was amazed at the types of people, who placed these orders, and even more so at the money I was making and that changed hands for these underground deals. This was the type of job that I excelled at and was able to hone a great many of my skills and appreciations during this happy time in my life.

But spending more and more time with her and being involved so deeply and darkly in her life, it began to feel like a partnership, like the team I never felt I had in my marriage and the companionship I didn't really think would be out there for me. It became a knotted feeling in my stomach on the days when I couldn't see her or thought she may be with someone else. I didn't recognise it for what it was. I couldn't have known how it would feel; there was no point of reference for me. Experience had not taught me love and I did not afford it time or attention in my mind, it was a myth of movies and legends.

But then I fell, so completely, utterly and madly in love with her. And I felt it, all the emotions that had been dormant in me for so long suddenly finding their way through. But it's not just as simple as that, love can cause undeniable happiness and pain all in one go, but the floodgates are then open, you do not choose what to feel of where it goes and it can save you or consume you. It consumed me, I did not think I was repressed by that point, rather just the opposite; I believed that I was astute and observant of my own desires and wants but had overlooked the obvious lack of love in my life. This oversight meant I had to recalculate so many assumptions I had made about myself but while taken by the demoness of love I had no chance.

I now felt I needed her, more than anything else and succumbed to the lack of eating, sleeping and non-cohesive thinking that an overwhelming feeling like this helps to create. I knew I was obsessed but couldn't shake it, knew it must run its course but didn't want to be playing anymore when it was my own feelings and life slipping away from me. She knew she had me though and tried to take me down the dark path she was on, to try and lead me fully into her world. But I was only a trophy to her, another man to break and cast aside in her pursuit of control and wanton pleasures.

There was a darker snuff side to the sex trade that I had try to stay away from but couldn't help being on the edges of. She had not tried to stay away from it, finding more lucrative ways to keep herself busy and there was obviously a lot more money involved but that's not what I was here for. She had more darkness than me so I knew it had to end, I would have to take the new emotional pain I felt and move on. But the impact of this experience has lasted and carried me through to my now matured tastes and aspirations, to keep me learning about people and I am never disappointed. To meet ones counterpart and have for a brief time that feeling of being a team was intense and potentially dangerous, I knew to back away eventually, but a lesser man may not have. Devious and calculating where I did not even think to go. A great friend and compadre in some dark times and plans in my life, but not to remain it seemed.

DEMONS AND DARKNESS

I have met so many people wrestling with their demons; it can be actually be quite heartbreaking to be in the company of someone who seems broken and completely destroyed by their burdens and desires. To know they have succumbed to the overwhelming input of the emotional senses and haven't made it through entirely, maybe the ones who weren't ready to wake up and process the reality that lay before them.

But I felt I didn't share their confusion or discomfort over what I was in the same way. I did not feel the need to raise the bar or try to go too far within my pursuits. Murder was a line I did not cross intentionally and will carry that darkness with me forever, but it was never a demon I had to burden my life with. I feel a connection to my subjects, they are not just objects. I have a certain moral and clinical obligation to them; I am a scientist conducting research after all.

There can be such darkness in people though, stand alone darkness that doesn't always have a demon. A free spirited dark that seems to penetrate their very soul and leads them forward in their lives. But I saw true dark surrounding the boy at school and taking over his soul, his obsessions ran so deep they were showing through. I felt it first then saw the torment following the stalk and kill from my younger years, an oppressive cloud that consumed and drove him I had to presume. He looked like he had lost the fight for control and was being puppeteered by the devil himself. I felt I was a different level to these examples, two extremes but the best I can think of. I felt more grounded and logical about my condition; I was able to go about my usual life, job, hobbies, rituals and family catch ups like everyone else. Friends to attend dinner parties with or discuss politics, economics and society at large, catch a film at the cinema or just relax. I do still have some demons though, it would be improper of me to try and sit on a throne of all knowing and pretend otherwise. Some things that I cannot entirely conclude or reconcile with yet, things that ware away at my soul. They're just not the same as everyone else's.

For most people though, it is hard to know how to keep your head clear enough to see the world you live in as well as take part. This can be a massive conflict of interest for the Stalker if not assimilated properly. I am more of a thinker even though I like doing and have taken in all the necessary information to make me a more skilled assailant, and I find no trouble now including in my 'normal' life what I thought I could never have.

Taking part is of upmost importance though, you can only watch for so long before you must do to really gain the valuable lesson waiting for you. Life doesn't happen without people, but to only take part is missing something so eloquent it almost destroys me when people don't notice it. It's the big Why. Why do we want what we want? I have definitely toiled and lost sleep over this one, in more ways than one, but I still find it can be elusive. Even to the well trained mind. Personal motive is everything, it defines your being, drives your passions and dictates your behaviour, yet so many know so little about it. No one can really tell you what it is; only you can know. Possibly.

These days as a psychiatrist I meet a great many people with personality issues and personal demons who carry with them a daily darkness, some I can help, some I can't, but I get something from all of them. Not honesty that's for sure, but it's when the lie runs so deep and has become self denial that I have the most productive results. I try not to stalk patients but it is difficult not to sometimes, I have intimate knowledge, their address and have spent enough time with them to have fantasized about doing certain things to them. Sometimes I am tempted and do cross the line and indulge a bit; mixing business and pleasure can go away a long away to cure what ails you in the workplace and relieve the stresses of the day. In fact, I had a new office girl start last week that I have plans for. The ground work has been laid, so tomorrow can be a knowing fear day I think.

But sex and by disposition often love, appears to be a very versatile thing, it can be used as a weapon, is a traded commodity, a human need, drives us to madness, despair, passion, revenge and many others in between. Yet we still seek it and want it although it can ultimately destroy us and leave us broken.

I have merely touched on the surface of a still very taboo but prevalent subject that is a big part of my life although leaves me with a label of society of sexual deviant (albeit given by myself), but that allows me to continue to explore my tastes and education surrounding them. But I understand there is more to cover, more delicious darkness to delve into that in my explanation of myself I may have neglected to provide you with. Already new questions have been raised and new experiments and theories need to be tested, but as they say no rest for the wicked…

ARE YOU A STALKER?

I am expecting the true stalker to already know the principles and motives of your actions and desires, but in case there are any left wondering about what you may be I have written an extra very simple section to determine if you are a stalker or harbour deviant potential stalker tendencies (just in case you are unsure).

If you like watching people, this makes you observant, a watcher. Not a stalker. If however, you imagine as you watch and observe, imagine the things you could be doing to that subject then you may have to assess yourself. To let your mind wander and imagine still doesn't make you a stalker, this could be merely casual daydreaming or lust raging out of control (also considered daydreaming). It's the quality and content of the imaginings that would consider you in the stalker fold. Only you will know of what I speak, if you do not then this book is possibly not for you, or stalking in fact. If you 'imagine' watching them from a distance, and following them to see where they live; then this is a good sign you have the tendencies and may want to improve your skills or seek professional assistance if you are not yet 'awake' enough to deal with it.

Stalkers will possess astute abilities to conceal their intentions – more commonly known as deception, ability to plan ahead and being hyper aware of people. They will also know what habit they are feeding, they will have to be honest with themselves at a minimum. Potential stalkers I would assume should have an inkling who they are. For the rest of you, I assume you're just curious and want to know more in your study of people. I commend you. Increasing knowledge of a potential predator can be a sign of looking out for yours or someone you care for's safety. It also gives me a slight thrill to know I am giving out this information, makes me feel like I am watching from the detention room again, but this time you know I am watching and can't do anything about it.

Printed in Great Britain
by Amazon